**DO NOT REMOVE
CARDS FROM POCKET**

AFFIRMATIVE
ACTION

AFFIRMATIVE ACTION

GERALDINE WOODS

AN IMPACT BOOK
NEW YORK • LONDON
TORONTO • SYDNEY
FRANKLIN WATTS • 1989

Photographs courtesy of: American Arbitration Association: p. 15;
UPI/Bettmann Newsphotos: pp. 19 (both), 25, 37 (top), 45, 51,
69, 111; AP/Wide World Photos: pp. 26, 37 (bottom), 40, 72;
Impact Visuals: p. 31 (Martha Tabor); Photo Researchers: pp. 43
(Leonard Lee Rue III), 48 (Arthur Tress).

Library of Congress Cataloging-in-Publication Data

Woods, Geraldine.
Affirmative action / by Geraldine Woods.
p.   cm. — (An Impact book)
Bibliography: p.
Includes index.
Summary: Describes the movement known as affirmative aciton which
seeks to prevent discrimination of human rights on th⸗ basis of sex
or race. Cites historical cases of discrimination and their impact
on affirmative action today.
ISBN 0-531-10657-8
1. Discrimination in employment—Law and legislation—United
States—Juvenile literature.   2. Affirmative action programs—Law
and legislation—United States—Juvenile literature.
[1. Discrimination in employment—Law and legislation.
2. Affirmative action programs—Law and legislation.]   I. Title.
KF3464.Z9W66   1989
342.73'087—dc19
[347.30287]   88-13872   CIP   AC

CONTENTS

1

WHAT IS AFFIRMATIVE ACTION?

Mary and John are applying for a job in the legal division of Multinational Corporation. Both are graduates of fine colleges; Mary achieved a solid B— average, and John was rated slightly higher. Mary attended one of the best law schools in the country and was ranked in the top third of her class. John's law-school record was similar. John worked for three summers as a clerk in his uncle's law firm. Mary, who had to help out at home with younger brothers and sisters, took some required courses during the summers so that she would have more free time during the school year. She has no legal experience.

Mary and John are both called for an interview. The personnel officer notes that each seems intelligent, hardworking, and well prepared. Because of John's work in a law firm and better grade-point average, Multinational's interviewer rates him slightly higher than Mary.

Who gets the job? That depends. For most of this century John would have been offered the job automatically, regardless of rating, because of two facts about Mary: She is a woman, and she is black. Until recently, few firms would have even considered hiring her, except perhaps as a secretary. (When Supreme Court Justice Sandra Day O'Connor was graduated from Stanford Law School in 1952, she ranked third in her class. Nevertheless, the law firm she applied to told her that they could only offer her the position of legal secretary because of her sex. Similar prejudice hindered minority groups.)

Today, however, the situation is somewhat different. Mary might well be offered the job, even though John ranks slightly higher, for precisely the same reasons she would have been rejected before. To make up for past discrimination, Multinational has instituted a plan to recruit women and minorities for its legal division. In hiring and promotion decisions, minority or female applicants might have a slight edge, though the plan specifies that no unqualified person may be selected solely because of race or sex. Also, if the company reduces its staff, no layoff may take race or sex into account.

A CONTROVERSIAL ISSUE

John, Mary, and the company they applied to are imaginary, but the program that affects their job possibilities—affirmative action—is not. Affirmative action refers to any steps taken by a company to increase the number and improve the rank of minority and female workers. It may include recruitment, training, hiring, promotion, and the assignment of business contracts. Affirmative action is also practiced by many public agencies such as police, fire, and sanitation as well as government departments like treasury, health, and tax. In addition, many universities and professional schools have affirmative action programs to increase the number of minority and female staff and students.

Affirmative action programs, which were begun only a

quarter century ago, are now operated by the majority of American companies. However, that they are widely used does not mean they are widely accepted. On the contrary, affirmative action may be one of the most controversial issues of recent years. These definitions of affirmative action reflect the passion of the argument:

> . . . a racial spoils system . . . It's demeaning because it says people are going to get ahead not because of what they can do, but because of their race.[1]
>> William Bradford Reynolds, assistant district attorney for civil rights during the Reagan years

> [a system] . . . to help produce a fairer distribution of income and opportunity, such as the distribution that presumably would exist today had there been an open and fairly competitive society all along.[2]
>> Richard F. America, writer on business and economic issues

> . . . state-sanctioned [approved] discrimination by reason of race.[3]
>> James J. Kilpatrick, political columnist

> . . . one of the few useful anti-discrimination techniques.[4]
>> editorial in *Nation* magazine

> affirmative racism[5]
>> Charles Murray, Manhattan Institute for Policy Research

[Programs that have] . . . made a difference where other measures have failed.[6]
> Rockefeller University,
> report on affirmative action
> around the world

. . . a way of helping people who are considered insufficiently capable of helping themselves.[7]
> Harvey Mansfield,
> Harvard University professor

. . . a legitimate method of pursuing a goal so important to the national welfare that it can be justified as a temporary policy for both public and private institutions.[8]
> Thomas Nagel,
> New York University professor

AFFIRMATIVE ACTION—IN ACTION

The system that all these people are arguing about is not a single program operated in the same way in every company, agency, and school. On the contrary, affirmative action plans differ tremendously. Some, like the imaginary Multinational plan, were established voluntarily. Others were instituted by court order to correct abuses of civil rights. Still others were designed to fulfill federal regulations for companies doing business with the government of the United States.

The target groups also differ from region to region, depending on the population of the area. Women, blacks, Hispanics, and American Indians are the most frequent participants. Asian-Americans are also part of some plans. Whom to include, like every other aspect of affirmative action, is the subject of a raging dispute. Some people favor helping only those individuals who are actually proven victims of discrimination. Others believe that all members of an affected group are entitled to consideration.

Another point of controversy is how to determine when discrimination exists. Affirmative action plans often rely on statistics to prove discrimination. Companies working for the federal government, for example, must analyze their work forces to determine which areas have very low percentages of minority and women workers compared to the proportion of these workers in the surrounding area. The company then estimates a reasonable increase it may achieve in a certain time period. Supporters of affirmative action believe this is a justifiable remedy for discrimination; in their view a 2 percent black work force in an area with a 25 percent black population must be the result of prejudice. Opponents disagree, saying that underrepresentation may have many causes—individual career preferences, differences in job training, family tradition, and so forth. To opponents, affirmative action based only on statistics is not justice but social engineering—arranging society to conform to a specific ideal.

The design of affirmative action plans may include extra recruitment: An employer or a college admissions officer may visit predominantly female or minority schools or place ads in magazines and newspapers popular with the targeted groups. A company might establish a program for its own employees to help prepare them for promotion to higher-paid positions. Hiring and promotion goals, as described above, are also widely used. If a court has determined that the company is guilty of serious discrimination over a period of years, quotas may be imposed. A quota is much stricter than a goal; a company need only demonstrate that it has made an effort to achieve a goal, but a quota must be met or the court has the power to order penalties.

Because affirmative action plans vary to such a degree, the best way to understand them is to look at a few.

Recruitment • About two hundred medical students found letters in their mailboxes recently from the Associated Medical Schools of New York, a group that represents thirteen New York State teaching hospitals. The association wrote to these students, who were all black, Puerto Rican, Mexican-American, or American Indian, to recruit them for further medical training in New York State. The students were former New Yorkers in their third year of medical school in other states. The association hoped to increase the number of minority doctors practicing in New York. Hispanics and blacks made up 26 percent of New York's population, yet according to the state health department, fewer than 10 percent of the residents training in New York hospitals in the mid-1980s belonged to minority groups, as did 8 percent of the state's licensed physicians. "The evidence . . . [shows] . . . that more than 80% of the doctors practicing in New York have also had their training in New York," explained a spokesman for the health department. "So it's enormously important that we increase the number of minorities in residencies here."[9]

COLLEGE AND GRADUATE ADMISSIONS

12. (Optional. You may omit this question if you wish.) Race or Ethnic Background: check one.
    Caucasian   ( )
    Black   ( )
    Hispanic   ( )
    Asian   ( )
    Native American   ( )

In the early 1970s, some form of the above question began to appear on many college and professional-school admission forms. To increase minority enrollment, admissions officers often award extra consideration to members of those groups. Legally no one may be accepted solely because of his or her race, sex, or ethnic background. Nevertheless, these factors may be considered a "plus" in a student's application. In many universities, members of minority groups are accepted even if their test scores are lower than those of rejected white applicants. At Georgetown Law Center, for example, the average minority scores are about a hundred points lower than those of white students.[10]

Robbie (last name withheld), a white high school senior, has applied to six colleges. He is a good student, with B+ grades and above-average scores on the Scholastic Aptitude Test (SAT). Robbie would like to go to Princeton, but even with his strong record he is not sure he will be accepted by such a competitive college. "It would help me if I were a member of a minority group," Robbie explains, "and I think that's unfair. People should be judged only on their records, not on the color of their skin."[11]

Training for Careers • An employee is angry. Everyone in the printing plant where he works traditionally receives a Christmas bonus. However, when he eagerly opens his pay envelope, only the usual amount is inside. The supervisor explains that because the worker has been absent frequently, he will not receive a gift.

The union is concerned, but management is firm. Tension grows. Everyone wants to settle the issue before it affects work at the plant. The solution? Both sides agree on an arbitrator—a neutral party who will hear the arguments and make a decision.

Although the printing case is imaginary, real incidents like it happen every day. What is unusual about the printing case, however, is that it was set before a class of student arbitrators so that they could practice their negotiating skills.

Even more unusual, the class was made up of fourteen blacks and Hispanics.[12]

The most common route to becoming a labor arbitrator is to apprentice oneself to someone in the field. This requires "connections" to people who have already established a career. It's not surprising, therefore, that groups traditionally outside the power structure have found it hard to break in. Out of 3,400 arbitrators listed with the American Arbitration Association (AAA), only 20 are *not* white males.[13]

Hezekiah Brown, a respected leader in the field, offers this special training course, which is sponsored by two universities and the AAA. The class members attend workshops and participate in mock hearings such as the one concerning the Christmas bonus. They also meet with people who may actually be their future employers—union and business executives.[14]

Training for a Job Test • Ken Wong, a Chinese-American, is a correction officer—a guard in a California jail. Ken got his job with the help of a group called Chinese for Affirmative Action (CAA), which recruits Asian-Americans for jobs in the prison system and other fields. CAA provided Ken with information about job openings and tutored him in skills needed for the Department of Correction exam. For six weeks Ken got up each day at 4:30 A.M. He trained in physical fitness, studied prison rules, and learned to handle firearms. Ken passed the test easily. During his first few months on the job, Ken received extra training from CAA and the Department of Corrections. CAA works with the Department of Corrections and other employers to increase the number of Asian-Americans in various careers. Like Ken, other members of the program believe that CAA helps them to qualify for better, more secure jobs than they would normally be eligible for.[15]

Hezekiah Brown (front row, second from left) stands proudly with graduates of his minority labor arbitrator program. Eleven black and Hispanic students successfully completed the course. They were chosen from among eighty applicants, based on their educational qualifications and experience in labor-management relations.

Hiring • Martin Goldman and Paul Lammermeier are qualified professors of Afro-American history. Early in their careers, both men received several job offers from various universities. Then, about 1972, Goldman and Lammermeier suddenly found themselves unemployed with no job prospects at all. Lammermeier eventually took a job as a short-order cook in an Ohio restaurant because he could not find academic employment.

Both men believe that affirmative action was the cause of their misfortune. In 1972 the Department of Health, Education, and Welfare (HEW) issued affirmative action guidelines. Colleges and universities receiving federal funds were to file affirmative action reports, and those with low numbers of minority and female professors were to design programs to increase representation of those groups. Almost overnight, qualified black professors of Afro-American history and other subjects were in great demand. Goldman and Lammermeier, white men, were not.[16]

Hiring by Court Order • One out of one thousand. That's the ratio of black to white clerical workers that existed in seven large agencies of the Alabama state government in the late 1960s. In semiprofessional and supervisory jobs, there were only twenty-six minority employees and over two thousand whites. This is in spite of the fact that during the 1960s, 25 percent of all Alabamans were black.

It's easy to see how this situation occurred. Alabama has a long history of racial segregation, and civil rights laws have made only a small dent in traditional practices. The state agencies routinely passed over blacks who appeared at the top of employment lists in favor of lower-ranked whites. This state also advertised available jobs only in white schools and media.

After a lawsuit, Judge Frank Johnson ordered Alabama to follow its hiring lists strictly, and he required that job offers be made to all those who could prove that they had been passed over because of discrimination. Over the next few years, however, minority employment in the seven agencies remained extremely low. There was one notable exception. The judge had ordered a quota for temporary workers: Twenty-five percent of all those hired for these jobs were to be members of minority groups. In one year the quota was met. In a separate lawsuit, quotas were also given to the Alabama state troopers because of proven discrimination. The state police also integrated.[17]

The U.S. Justice Department, noting the increased employment for blacks under quotas and the lack of change in agencies without quotas, decided to go back to court. Justice attorneys asked for hiring quotas in the seven Alabama agencies. The judge said no, but he urged the agencies to use fair hiring policies. Two years later the situation was unchanged. This time the judge issued a decision finding statewide discrimination. He did not order quotas, but he did say that if progress was not made in one year, quotas would be the only possible relief. Alabaman government departments began to integrate almost immediately. Today 20 percent of these government workers are minorities, and blacks appear in nearly all job categories.[18]

Hiring by Consent Decree • The Associated Press (AP), the giant news service that provides worldwide coverage for newspapers, instituted an affirmative action plan in 1983. In the early 1970s seven female journalists had sued AP, charging that women were denied opportunity in the company. Minority workers also supplied evidence of discrimination by the news service.

After ten years in and out of court, AP signed a consent decree—a legal agreement approved by the court. About a million dollars was shared by women who had been denied employment or promotions, and a smaller amount went to minority employees. The company also set hiring and promotion goals for these groups for a period of five years, established a job-posting system to better publicize openings, and created a summer intern program for college students. After only one year, the percentage of women and minorities hired by AP increased dramatically.[19]

Promotions—Voluntary Plan • The Fourth of July is an all-American holiday, marked by barbecues, fireworks, and for many people, the all-American sport of baseball. Independence Day of 1987, however, was almost without its traditional game. Jesse Jackson had threatened to organize a boycott of major league parks unless baseball started promoting more minority people to administrative and managerial jobs. Jackson's effort was sparked by a statement made in April 1987 by Al Campanis, who was then vice-president of the Los Angeles Dodgers. Campanis was asked by a talk-show host why there were so few blacks in the most responsible baseball jobs. (Although 25 percent of the players are members of minority groups, there have been only three black managers and one black general manager in baseball's long history.) Campanis replied that blacks might not have "some of the necessities" for these positions. An uproar followed these remarks, and civil rights leaders, along with black players such as Dave Winfield and Don Baylor, called for an affirmative action program in the major leagues.

The baseball commissioner hired Dr. Harry Edwards, a black professor from the University of California, to head the program. Edwards's job was to identify blacks and Hispanics with major league experience who might fill front office or managerial jobs. Satisfied that an effort was being made, Jackson called off the boycott. In the following months a few members of minority groups were offered jobs. One was Michael Wilson, who became controller of the Detroit Tigers. Wilson told reporters that he was sure his race had something to do with his hiring. However, he added that the best way he could answer questions about his ability was "to do a good job."[20]

Promotions—Court Settlement • As a young man, Edward Harris played bit parts on Broadway and on television. In 1954, he began to look for more stable work. Harris found a job with the Long Island Railroad, using his clear

Above: *following a meeting with Baseball Commissioner Peter Ueberroth, Jesse Jackson explains the details of a proposed timetable and enforcement procedures to ensure the hiring of minorities in baseball's upper management positions.* Below: *former Dodger vice-president Al Campanis shortly after retiring due to controversial statements he made about blacks in baseball.*

actor's voice to announce trains. Eventually he rose to the position of assistant station manager at Pennsylvania Station in New York City. However, according to Harris, something was wrong. During his years with the railroad Harris believed that he saw many instances of discrimination against blacks. In his view, far too few blacks were promoted to supervisory positions, and many were locked into low-paying jobs by restrictive rules.

In 1972, Harris and six other minority workers filed suit against the railroad. Fifteen years, over a million documents, and thousands of hours of testimony later, the case was settled out of court. The railroad agreed to create a career opportunity center where all employees could seek transfers to better-paying jobs. In addition, the Long Island Railroad promised to establish training centers. Under the terms of the settlement, the centers could be open to all who applied or, if entrance were restricted, could accept an equal number of blacks and whites for a period of four years. The railroad also agreed to post notice of all job openings and to give first preference to current employees seeking a better position.[21]

Set-Asides • Recently the California Assembly approved a $5 billion bond issue in order to finance public projects in that state. Bond issues are organized by investment firms, which receive a fee for their services. The California bonds followed a growing trend toward affirmative action in finance: The assembly stated that there must be a good-faith effort to sell at least 20 percent of the bonds through firms owned by minorities or women. Laws like these, which reserve a certain amount of business for minority- or female-owned firms, are called "set-asides."

The W. R. Lazard Company is one of the firms that may benefit from the California bond issue. W. R. Lazard was founded by Wardell Lazard, a black man with experience in investment banking and with many contacts in state and local governments around the country. The W. R. Lazard Company often handles business from cities that have "set aside" a certain amount of work either by law or informally. Lazard himself is pleased with the growth of his company, but he hopes to move beyond the label of "minority company." "I know that my niche in this business has been my ability to work with cities that had minority mayors," he explains, "but our aim is to be a highly-professional firm that just happens to be minority-owned."[22]

All the plans described above have created winners and losers: For every person who gets a job, a promotion, or a spot in college, there is another who is rejected. Perhaps that is why affirmative action programs are so controversial. Opponents sense a basic unfairness; supporters believe that past discrimination more than justifies affirmative action today. James Farmer, a leader in the black civil rights movement, may have summed up the controversy better than anyone. "Very often the issues [of civil rights today] are right versus right," he said. "Affirmative action is one such issue."[23]

2

DISCRIMINATION IN AMERICAN HISTORY

"We hold these truths to be self-evident, that all men are created equal." That statement from the Declaration of Independence is the first thing almost every schoolchild learns about America, and in some ways it's the very foundation of our democracy. Yet even a quick glance at history reveals that equality has never actually been reached in the United States. Women and blacks were not included in the founding fathers idea of "all men." For many years, neither were Hispanics, Asians, or American Indians.

WOMEN

The *New York Times* of August 26, 1963, listed jobs in its classified section under "Help Wanted—Male" and "Help Wanted—Female." According to these ads, men could apply for work as engineers, insurance-claim representatives, boiler inspectors, assistant managers, and clerks. Women could seek positions as receptionists, "girl Fridays," secretaries, dental hygienists, and so forth. Most of the ads for men indicated that the employer would train the new worker or cited "excellent career opportunities." The ads for women mentioned no career possibilities at all.

The *Times* ads illustrate the centuries of separation between "woman's work" and "a man's job." For most of our history definite types of work were open to each sex, and few positions were considered suitable for both. The *Times* of August 26 listed only one job—cashier—open to either men or women. The ad was printed in the section for men.

This separation was largely due to traditional roles for men and women, often learned from parents and reinforced by society. The male jobs reflect the idea that men are active—the doers and thinkers, the breadwinners for their families. The female jobs were mostly supporting positions, mirroring the subordinate role women traditionally played in our society. As non-career jobs, the women's work was also more temporary, because women were viewed as working only to "help out" the primary workers, the men in their families. It was assumed that married women, and particularly those with children, would make their homes and families their life's work.

These beliefs have always been at least partly incorrect; nevertheless, they have been a powerful force in shaping our society. At times, the traditional roles were even enforced by law. In 1873, for example, a woman named Bradwell wanted to practice law in Illinois, but a state law reserved that career for men. Bradwell challenged this, but the Supreme Court ruled against her, stating that "the natural and proper timidity and delicacy which belongs to the female sex evidently unfits it for many occupations of civil life."[1]

Other laws prohibited women from jobs ranging from bartending to newspaper delivery.[2] Also, married women at times were the subject of special legislation. During the Depression, the federal government would not employ a woman if her husband already had a civil service job.[3] Until 1940, married women were not allowed to teach in most states.[4]

Some of the laws were designed to protect women from heavy labor or long hours. Critics point out that these laws generally offered little protection at all; they simply shunted women into "female" fields with lower salaries. A 1910 law barred women from jobs as night clerks in hotels. However, without violating the law, women could—and did—scrub hotel floors all night at a much lower wage.[5] Other laws prohibiting women from heavy lifting did not apply to hospitals, where nurses' aides routinely lifted adult patients and where they earned much less than male factory workers.[6]

Interestingly, almost all these laws and customs were suspended whenever the nation needed women's work. In World Wars I and II, women were recruited to fill jobs left vacant by soldiers. Newspapers presented pictures of women operating blast furnaces and other heavy machinery as part of the war effort. Advertising from the World War II era featured "Rosie the Riveter," a patriotic character who worked in a factory. Real "Rosies" numbered about 8 million.[7]

After each period of national emergency, women were fired to make way for returning veterans, even though most wanted to continue with their jobs. A survey taken after World War II showed that 80 percent of women workers preferred to keep their positions in peacetime.[8]

The idea of separate spheres of interest for each sex also influenced education. Until the end of the nineteenth century, there were almost no high schools or colleges for women; girls were to receive their training at home—usually preparing them only to be housewives and mothers. After the Civil War the first women's colleges were established. Professional schools remained off-limits for much longer.

Women workers during World War II take a break
from work to eat lunch. They were working on
the world's longest airplane assembly line.

Elizabeth Blackwell, the first woman doctor in the United States, was turned down by medical schools throughout the country before being admitted to Geneva Medical College in New York State in the late nineteenth century. Columbian College of Law in 1887 stated that it would not admit women because "coeducation would distract the students" and "women had not the mentality to study law."[9] By the early twentieth century, few medical or law schools completely barred women, but as late as 1920 most had a 5 percent quota for female students.[10]

In 1964, a law prohibiting sex discrimination in many areas of American life was passed. However, separate want ads such as those in the *New York Times* were printed for several more years. Even after sex-based ads were dropped, sex discrimination continued, as it continues today. It takes more than a law to change people's inner feelings and society's long-standing customs. Even in the 1980s, women who apply for jobs in fields traditionally closed to them have often reported that the doors remain just as firmly shut. A survey by the *National Law Journal* reported that 40 percent of associates hired in 1986 and 1987 were women. However, only about one out of every thirteen partners (the highest position in law firms) were female. The study found that women are moving into partnership at a much lower rate than men with the same experience.[11] Furthermore, in 1986 only 1.7 percent of the corporate officers of the 500 largest American companies were women. Only one company in that group had a female chief executive officer, and she had inherited the business from her husband.[12] In a

Dr. Elizabeth Blackwell,
America's first woman doctor

1988 survey of 133 engineers, one-third of the women said they were bypassed for promotions in favor of less qualified men. (Only one man reported that the reverse had happened to him.)[13]

Sex discrimination in education also continues. In a recent survey, one-third of the female students in trade and industrial courses who were questioned reported that their guidance counselors had tried to discourage them from those studies.[14] In some school districts, girls are still required to take more home economics courses than their male classmates; the boys must spend more time in industrial training.[15] Other studies have found that many teachers subject female students to a number of discriminatory practices, even without realizing it. In class discussions girls are interrupted more and receive less time from the teacher than boys. Girls are more often praised for neatness and boys for the quality of their work.[16] No single practice discourages women and puts them in their "proper" place. Taken together, however, small acts of discrimination become a significant factor in women's achievement.

While barriers are now breaking down at a faster rate, it is still obvious from current statistics that the genders are not represented equally in most fields. The majority of all female workers are employed in 20 of the 421 job titles listed in a Department of Labor handbook. Moreover, over half of all women workers are employed in occupations that are 75 percent female.[17]

Table 1 lists statistics on women's role in some occupations.[18]

Segregation by sex may prevent women from seeking work that interests them; it also has important economic consequences. Occupations that are predominantly female have always paid less than those that are predominantly male. Eighty percent of all female workers are in the twenty

TABLE 1

Occupation	Percent Who Are Women
Total work force	44.4
Doctors	17.6
Nurses	94.3
Lawyers	18.0
Elementary schoolteachers	85.2
Sales supervisors	30.5
Sales clerks	68.6
Firefighters	1.9
Police and detectives	10.9
Cleaners	41.5
Construction workers	2.8
Dentists	1.8
Waiters	91.1

lowest-paid careers.[19] This is not an accident. Statistics show that when women enter a particular profession, a significant number of men leave it and the average salary drops. Between 1960 and 1980, for example, the percentage of female radio operators rose from 17 percent to 57 percent. The median salary for this work during the same period dropped from 8 percent above to 33 percent below the average male wage.[20]

Even in fields where men and women are mixed, many women are paid less than their male counterparts.[21] Although unequal pay for the same work is illegal, many employees can and do get around the law. In firms in which salaries are negotiated separately, workers may not always be aware of what their colleagues are earning. This may allow for differences in male and female wages. In other businesses, men and women doing similar work are given different job titles (such as nurse's aide and orderly), with the male job drawing the higher salary.

Women are also clustered in the lowest positions in many companies. In a typical firm, the secretaries, receptionists, and assistants are mainly female, while the majority of supervisors and executives are male. There are a number of reasons for this. Women are more likely than men to be recent additions to the work force; naturally they begin with entry-level jobs. Because of pregnancy and family responsibilities, women often have interrupted work histories. This makes it difficult to move up the career ladder.

Nevertheless, discrimination is still a factor. One study compared the salaries of unmarried men and women who had worked for a similar amount of time. The women earned only about 65 percent of the average wage of men the same age.[22] Comparing all workers (married and unmarried), women in 1987 earn about 68 percent as much as men.[23] To put it another way, even in the 1980s female college graduates earn only slightly more than male high school dropouts.[24]

Apart from wages, sexism has affected female finances in other ways. For much of our history women were legally required to turn over all their property to their husbands upon marriage. If the husband mismanaged the property or even gave it away, the wife was powerless. Married women could not legally go into business, make contracts, or sue for payment of debts.[25] Although this is not now the case, these practices have contributed to the fact that American men control more of the nation's investment money than women. Partly for this reason, fewer women than men have had the money to start their own businesses or buy stock in others.

In many offices women are still more likely than men to be secretaries, receptionists, and assistants.

BLACKS

Three hundred and fifty billion dollars. That's the value of the property and labor one economist estimates was taken from blacks throughout U.S. history because of racial discrimination.[26] This discrimination began even before the United States became an independent country. From the sixteenth century onward, blacks brought from Africa were sold as farm and house slaves. On the small farms of New England, slaveholding was not profitable, but the free labor quickly became a great economic asset on the large plantations of the South, and slavery became entrenched there.

In the eyes of the law, slaves were considered property, not people, and were treated as such. This is obvious in the slave codes, a set of rules that governed slaves during the colonial days. Slaves were forbidden to leave the plantations without their masters' permission; they were not allowed to marry and could be bought and sold without regard to family ties. Slaves received no wages for their work beyond the survival level of room and board.[27]

The revolutionary period brought no improvement for blacks. The original American constitution viewed slaves as property, counting each as three-fifths of a white person in apportioning representatives. Moreover, many state laws held that slaves could not vote, hold office, learn to read and write, own property or firearms, do business, testify in court against a white, make contracts, marry, or hold meetings without the presence of a white. Striking a white was grounds for the death penalty, but the murder of a slave was a minor crime. At times it was even legal; slaves caught escaping in some states could be executed on the spot without a trial.[28]

The small number of free blacks in early America were also denied equal rights. In the South, free blacks were prohibited from various trades and schools and could not travel without a special pass. In Georgia, free blacks were not even allowed to own property. Free blacks in the North were not much better off; they could not vote in many states and constantly faced discrimination in employment. Some northern states had laws prohibiting blacks from various careers; others simply turned blacks away from "unsuitable" jobs. In many northern states, blacks were not allowed in public schools.[29]

Although slavery was abolished after the Civil War, blacks in the South received little economic benefit from emancipation. Since slaves had not been allowed to accumulate property, freed blacks had absolutely nothing when the war ended. The only way many could survive was to become sharecroppers—farmers who rented the land they farmed and gave the owner of the land a portion of their harvest as payment for the use of that land. The catch was that the sharecroppers had to borrow money for tools, seed, and other items from their landlord, usually at very high rates. The tenants were almost always in debt; therefore, they could not leave their farms. Sharecropping became another type of slavery.[30] Also, white unions and management excluded most blacks from skilled trades; former slaves found that only the most menial jobs were available to them. Furthermore, since it had been illegal for slaves to learn to read and write, about 90 percent of the nation's blacks were illiterate when the Civil War ended.[31] Many jobs were closed to them by this lack of education.

The southern states also enacted Black Codes, rules meant to keep blacks in an inferior position. The earlier prohibitions against carrying guns, testifying in court, and so forth were continued. Most codes also regulated what type of work blacks could do and how they could buy and sell property. Here is an example from Opelousas, Louisiana:

No Negro or freedman shall be allowed to come within the limits of the town . . . without special permission from his employer, specifying the object of his visit and the time necessary for [the work].[32]

In many areas "vagrancy laws" also reduced blacks to a kind of slavery; a black traveling without a pass could be arrested. For punishment, the black was hired out to the highest bidder, with the salary going to the government as a fine.[33] Also, black children from poor families could be apprenticed to whites until the child reached adulthood if government officials decided that the parents could not provide for their children. The parents and children had no say in the matter, and no wages were paid. A South Carolina law summarized the feelings of most southerners: To give full rights to blacks, it declared, was "treason to race."[34]

The U.S. government passed the Thirteenth, Fourteenth, and Fifteenth constitutional amendments shortly after the Civil War, attempting to give equal rights to blacks. (The Thirteenth Amendment ended slavery, the Fourteenth guaranteed blacks "equal protection under the law," and the Fifteenth secured voting rights.) Nevertheless, the segregation enforced by the Black Codes remained in effect for over eighty years. During that period the Supreme Court ruled that segregation was legal as long as the facilities were "separate but equal." In reality, all-black accommodations were very far from equal. In 1929, for example, the average white school in the South received ten times as much funding as the average black school.[35] In border states (those located a little farther north), the ratio was two to one.[36] As a result of this, most black schools had fewer teachers, substandard school buildings, out-of-date texts, and so forth.

Conditions for black education in the North were somewhat better, but still unequal. Moreover, job discrimination was just as brutal in the North, with blacks being considered only for the lowest jobs. Throughout the United States in 1900, 84 percent of all blacks worked on farms or as servants and unskilled laborers.[37] This pattern continued unchanged well into the twentieth century.

Although a few unions accepted blacks, most did not. Thus, the organizations fighting for the rights of workers fought mainly for whites. Even those blacks who were members of unions found their rights seldom upheld. In 1903, for example, a black bricklayer in Indiana went to work on a new job one morning and found that all his white co-workers had gone on strike rather than work with him. The contractor fired the black, who appealed to the union. The union turned down his appeal and fined the black twenty-five dollars for working at a nonunion job while the union was considering his case.[38]

Blacks were also treated unequally by many government agencies. During the Depression, the average black family received about nine dollars in benefits for every fifteen dollars a white family was given.[39] The early minimum wage and social security laws did not apply to farm laborers, servants, cooks, and yard workers—occupations with large concentrations of blacks.[40] Various programs for farmers, intended to tide them over during bad years, did not apply to blacks. During World War I, for example, southern white farmers were allowed to store their cotton in state warehouses until trade with Europe resumed. Blacks received no such help, and many went bankrupt.[41] In recent years the U.S. Commission on Civil Rights reported that there was discrimination against blacks in all the programs run by the Farmers Home Administration.[42]

In 1954, the Supreme Court heard a landmark case, *Brown* v. *the Board of Education* of Topeka, Kansas. A black lawyer named Thurgood Marshall, who was eventually named to the Supreme Court himself, argued that the "separate but equal" doctrine was unjust. The court agreed and in a series of decisions outlawed segregation and discrimination in many forms. For the first time in U.S. history, blacks were truly equal in the eyes of the law. However, legal equality was still far from actual equality. During the 1960s the civil rights movement, led by Martin Luther King, Jr., and others, pressed for reform. As the nation watched on television, blacks sat down at "whites only" lunch counters and walked to work rather than ride on segregated buses. Peaceful demonstrators and some rioters gave the message over and over: Blacks must be equal.

Some modern polls have shown that white Americans believe that blacks now have every opportunity available to whites, and that racial prejudice is a thing of the past. However, polls of blacks disagree, and statistics support this view.[43]

School segregation has been illegal for over thirty years, yet in the early 1980s nearly one-half of black elementary and high school pupils attended schools with over 99 per-

Above: *black students stage a demonstration against "whites only" lunch counters.* Below: *nearly empty classrooms were a result of a 1964 boycott to protest segregation in Boston's public schools. 10,000 black and white children boycotted the public schools in response to the call of civil rights leaders to boycott those schools.*

cent minority enrollment. During the same time period, only 35 percent of black elementary and high school students were in schools with more than 50 percent white enrollment. This pattern continued in higher education; 44 percent of black college students attended predominantly black schools.[44]

Moreover, many schools with more than 50 percent black enrollment still receive less money and have inferior facilities than mostly white schools. A recent report on New York City public schools, for example, found that the city's school districts with large concentrations of minority students are underfunded compared with those districts that are mostly white.[45] Moreover, blacks are still underrepresented in higher education: They make up 12 percent of the nation's population but only 8 percent of its college students.[46]

Black employment also remains unequal. In the mid-1980s over fifty thousand charges of discrimination a year were filed with the Equal Employment Opportunity Commission (EEOC), many by blacks.[47] While each charge is not proof of prejudice, the huge number is evidence of a continuing problem. Furthermore, the unemployment rate for blacks is approximately twice that of whites; for young black men it is three times the rate of whites.[48] Blacks are also scarce in high-salaried professional fields: only 4 percent of the nation's lawyers and 4 percent of its managers are black. However, blacks make up 50 percent of the country's maids and garbage collectors.[49]

These employment statistics are mirrored in salaries: The average income for black college graduates is only slightly more than that of white high school graduates. The average black family earns only about 57 percent as much as the average white family.[50] Forty-five percent of black children live in poverty, compared with 15 percent of white children.[51] There may be many causes for this: the number of single-parent households, level of education, and so forth. Nevertheless, discrimination plays a role.

AMERICAN INDIANS

Native Americans are included in many affirmative action programs for a number of reasons—the theft of their land, unjust treatment by the federal government's Bureau of Indian Affairs, and racial prejudice. These problems are evident in even a brief study of American history.

In 1839, for example, thousands of weary Indians arrived in what is now Oklahoma. The Indians, who were members of the Cherokee, Chickasaw, Choctaw, Creek, and Seminole tribes, had just signed a treaty with the government of the United States. Settlers had wanted the Indians' homelands in the East, and the Indians had been pressured to leave. The tribes, largely without horses and wagons, had been forced to walk all the way to the new Indian territory. It was a terrible journey; one-third of each tribe died along the way. Still, the government had promised the tribes their new land "as long as the grass grows and the waters run."

The grass still grows in Oklahoma, and the rivers still run, but the Indians there now own only a fraction of the land they were originally given. Little by little their territory was opened to white settlement, and the Indians were moved or forced onto smaller tracts of land. The Cherokees call their trip to Oklahoma from the Southeast the "trail of tears." Others sometimes see it as another step in the usual pattern of Indian history in the United States: the "trail of broken treaties."[52] From the earliest days of European settlement of the North American continent, Indian tribes were dispossessed of their lands. Although many fought for their homes, the Indians faced superior numbers and weapons and inevi-

Two Seneca Indian leaders look over the Kinzua Dam. Although the federal government granted the Senecas $15 million as compensation for constructing the power project on their land, the Indians will never again be able to use most of that land for their livelihood.

tably met with defeat. Many tribes signed treaties, as did the five Oklahoman tribes, only to find the terms changed whenever it was to the whites' advantage.

This is true even in modern times. In 1965 the Kinzua Dam was built on the Allegheny River. The dam produced electric power, provided facilities for water sports, and improved navigation. It also flooded 10,000 acres belonging to the Seneca Indians, leaving their reservation with only 2,300 acres of habitable land. The project directly violated a treaty the tribe had made with the federal government in the eighteenth century. When the army corps of engineers presented plans for the dam at a congressional hearing in the early 1960s, the treaty was deemed of so little importance that the tribe was not even invited to testify. In fact, they were not even informed that a hearing was being held.[53]

Losing land is an economic blow for any group. For many Indian tribes, however, the loss was nearly fatal, because the tribes' entire economy was linked directly to the land. Hunting, fishing, trapping, raising animals—these activities prosper only in certain areas, and only where there is a sufficient amount of land. The financial drain may be estimated from this statistic: American Indians now own less than 3 percent of the land they held when the white settlers arrived.[54]

The first Americans have also suffered in other ways. In 1824 the tribes were placed under the control of the Bureau of Indian Affairs, which deprived Indians of most powers of self-government. The bureau, run largely by non-Indians, was often inefficient and corrupt. Although it was charged with safeguarding Indian interests, the bureau often favored the needs of the nation's white majority—at the expense of the Indians. An example of this is leasing. Few tribes had the money to buy machinery or large amounts of livestock. Therefore, many tribes leased their water, grazing, farming, or mineral rights to others. The bureau often arranged the leases at very low rates. The Sioux tribe of the Dakotas, for example, received only a fraction of the price for grazing rights that ranchers routinely paid when renting from whites.[55]

Indians seeking employment outside the reservation also faced many obstacles. Too many Americans agreed with President Theodore Roosevelt, who said, "I don't go as far as to think that the only good Indians are the dead Indians, but I believe nine out of ten are, and I shouldn't inquire too closely into the case of the tenth."[56] Stereotypes of laziness, dishonesty, drunkenness, or savagery were common throughout much of our history and are partly to blame for the fact that the rate of unemployment for Indians was sometimes ten times that of whites.

At present, Indians are the poorest minority in the country. The unemployment rate for Indians is about 35 percent; on some reservations it can reach 80 or 90 percent. The average Indian family's income is only one-third of the average white family's; on some reservations 80 percent of the Indians have incomes below the poverty line.[57]

ASIAN-AMERICANS

Earl Warren, former chief justice of the Supreme Court, once commented that "when we are dealing with members of the Caucasian (white) race we have methods that will test the loyalty of them . . . but when we deal with the Japanese we are in an entirely different field and we cannot form any opinion that we believe to be sound."[58] This comment echoes the racial stereotype that has plagued Asian-Americans since the first wave of Asian immigrants arrived in the United States a little over a hundred years ago. Too often,

Poor Indian children in a rural village

whites have viewed people of Asian descent as deceitful and hard to understand.

The consequences of this prejudice have been serious. During World War II, for example, Japanese-Americans living on the West Coast were ordered to leave their homes and businesses and move to internment camps farther inland. Even those who were born in the United States and had never seen Japan were included in the order. German- and Italian-Americans, whose countries were also at war with the United States, were never interned. After the war the interned Japanese were freed; the value of the property and businesses they had lost was estimated at $400 million. No price could be placed on the emotional trauma they had suffered.

Earlier, prejudice against Chinese people had resulted in the Chinese Exclusion Act of 1882, which limited Chinese immigration to the United States.[59] Many Chinese had come to "the land of the golden mountain" (California) in the mid-nineteenth century. Employers were glad to hire the Asians as railroad, factory, and farm workers, especially since most Chinese were paid far less than whites doing the same work. However, white workers feared the competition for their jobs. Many bloody riots occurred in the 1870s and 1880s; during one in Denver in 1880, every Chinese home and business in the city was destroyed. Around this time a man named Denis Kearney organized the American Workingman's Party in California. Their slogan was "The Chinese must go!"[60]

Many laws, like the Chinese Exclusion Act, were passed in the late nineteenth and early twentieth centuries to restrict immigration from Asia.[61] Other laws regulated Asian-American life in the United States. Until 1873, for example, Chinese in California were not allowed to testify in court. Some discrimination was more subtle. The city of San Fran-

Japanese-Americans in an
internment camp in California

cisco once made a practice of denying licenses to Chinese-owned laundries. The reason given was fire hazard: The laundries were built of wood. However, wooden laundries owned by whites had no trouble receiving licenses.[62]

In recent years immigrants from Vietnam, Cambodia, and other Asian countries have also faced prejudice. However, many Asian-Americans have reached high levels of achievement: The average educational level and family income of Asian-Americans is higher than the national average, and this has also resulted in prejudice against the group.

HISPANIC-AMERICANS

Such achievement is not, unfortunately, true of Hispanic-Americans—people whose ancestors came from Mexico, Puerto Rico, Cuba, and other Spanish-speaking countries. There are currently about 12 million Hispanics in the United States; in a recent year their average family income was only about two-thirds of the average income of a white family. Approximately 29 percent of Hispanic-Americans live below the poverty line, including over 40 percent of all Hispanic children under the age of six.[63] In the first quarter of 1987, 9.7 percent of Hispanic-American workers were unemployed (compared to 5.9 percent in the nation as a whole.)[64] Finally, 71 percent of Hispanic-American students attend predominantly minority schools. Almost one-third attend schools in which at least nine out of ten students are members of minority groups.[65]

These statistics are similar to those of blacks, and the cause of prejudice against Hispanic-Americans is also similar. During the early days of colonization by Spain, marriage between the races was common. Most Hispanics have white, black, and Indian blood. Their descendants' skin color varies; much discrimination is based on the darkness of skin, with darker people encountering more prejudice.

Although they are often viewed as a single people, Hispanic-Americans are actually members of several ethnic groups. Many Chicanos (Mexican-Americans) trace their ancestry back to the original settlers of the Southwest. When this area became part of the United States, the Mexicans who were living there were often forced off their land. Mexican deeds were sometimes stolen or burned, or property was seized for nonpayment of new taxes levied just to drive the Mexicans away.[66] The dispossessed Mexicans, as well as new immigrants from Mexico, often found work as migrant farm workers. Migrant work has traditionally paid very little, although the hours are long and the labor is brutally hard.

Even that labor was hard to get during the Depression, and a great deal of anti-Mexican feeling surfaced in California during the early 1930s. State social workers even came up with a plan to send Mexican-Americans "back" to Mexico (whether or not they had ever been there). Chicanos were offered free train fare if they would leave the United States; many, out of work and starving, accepted.[67]

Puerto Ricans became American citizens some years after their island was ceded to the United States by the treaty ending the Spanish-American War. Large numbers of Puerto Ricans, driven away by the poverty at home, settled in New York and other Northeastern cities. Puerto Ricans, like blacks, were often offered only the lowest-paying jobs because of lack of education, the language barrier, or discrimination. In 1950, 65 percent of Puerto Rican men were in unskilled or semiskilled employment in factories, hotels, restaurants, and the like.[68] In the same year, 80 percent of Puerto Rican women who had emigrated from Puerto Rico

were employed in factories and only 7 percent in clerical or sales jobs.[69] By the 1980s, more Puerto Ricans had moved into office, craft, and professional positions, but the numbers are still low.

In fact, Hispanics as a whole are still concentrated in lower-paying jobs. Nationally, Hispanic-Americans make up almost 5.4 percent of the work force, but only 2.2 percent of officials and managers, 1.9 percent of professionals (doctors, lawyers, etc.), and 3.5 percent of technicians. However, Hispanics account for about 7 percent of service workers (waiters, cooks, maids, etc.) and over 12 percent of the nation's laborers.[70]

In recent years, Hispanics have faced a new problem. According to a 1987 law, employers who hire illegal aliens (citizens of other countries who do not have permits to work in the United States) may be fined or even jailed. Since many illegal aliens are from Spanish-speaking countries, some employers are afraid to hire any people of Hispanic background. This generalization has cost many Hispanic-Americans their right to work.

Hispanics fight this prejudice, as blacks, women, and other groups have, with their own work, political pressure, and consciousness-raising. Nevertheless, the battle for equal rights is still raging.

A poor Hispanic neighborhood in New York City

3

THE HISTORY OF AFFIRMATIVE ACTION

Early in 1961 a bomb exploded in a church in Birmingham, Alabama, killing three little black girls attending services. The crime horrified the nation and particularly distressed President John F. Kennedy. At the same time, the civil rights movement was gaining momentum as blacks called attention to their plight and pressed for reform. Shortly after the bombing, Kennedy sent a civil rights bill to Congress. The bill was designed to outlaw discrimination on the basis of race, ethnic background, and religion.

Theoretically, President Kennedy's bill should not have been necessary. The Fourteenth Amendment to the Constitution, which was passed just after the Civil War, says that no state may "deny any person within its jurisdiction the equal protection of the law." Both blacks and whites should be treated equally under this amendment, but in 1961 blacks were anything but equal. Additional protection was clearly necessary. Perhaps the strongest proof of this is that Kennedy was worried about the chances for his bill on Capitol Hill. Employment was the touchiest topic; Kennedy omitted it from the bill because he thought that including it

Police examine the wreckage at the Sixth Avenue Baptist Church in Birmingham, Alabama, after a bomb explosion killed four black girls during Sunday School.

would mean certain defeat. Even without an employment provision, the bill could not get enough support in Congress to become law.

Nevertheless, like all presidents, Kennedy had the power to issue an executive order. An executive order is a law that comes straight from the president and does not have to be voted on by Congress. Kennedy's Executive Order 10925, issued on March 6, 1961, made a special requirement for all companies doing business with the federal government. It stated that:

> the contractor will not discriminate against any employee or applicant for employment because of race, creed, color, or national origin. The contractor will take *affirmative action* [italics added] to ensure that applicants are employed, and that employees are treated during employment, without regard to their race, creed, color, or national origin. Such action shall include, but not be limited to, the following: employment, upgrading, demotion or transfer; recruitment or recruitment advertising; layoff or termination; rates of pay or other forms of compensation; and selection for training, including apprenticeship.[1]

This was the first use ever of the term "affirmative action," and no one was totally sure what it meant. Since "affirmative" is "positive," the order seemed to call for an employer to go beyond passive or neutral behavior and take "action" to recruit, train, hire, and promote more minorities. Exactly how this was to be done was not explained.

The order also provided for a President's Commission on Equal Employment Opportunity (PCEEO) headed by the vice-president and staffed by representatives from agencies of the government that often gave contracts to private companies. The PCEEO was in charge of compliance; that is, it was to see that the executive order was actually carried out. The PCEEO required companies with federal contracts to file "compliance reports" showing that they were not discriminating. A company that did discriminate could lose its federal contracts and even be barred from future government work.[2]

Kennedy's executive order was well intentioned, but it did not go very far toward eliminating job discrimination. A study of ninety-one government contractors revealed an average of 5.0 percent minority employment in May 1961 and an average of only 5.1 percent in January 1963.[3] Part of the problem was that employers were not really expected to show results under Executive Order 10925. Compliance reports were just supposed to demonstrate a "good faith" effort to hire more minorities, a fairly difficult condition to evaluate. Penalties were therefore rare. In fact, not a single one was ever imposed on a major contractor under Kennedy's order. Furthermore, companies without federal contracts were not covered by the order, and sex discrimination was not mentioned.

THE CIVIL RIGHTS ACT OF 1964

By 1964, the movement for racial equality had gained more support, and a civil rights law was again introduced in Congress. Its titles, or parts, called for a ban on discrimination in public accommodations (hotels, restaurants, trains, etc.) and public education, federal programs, and employment. Title VII, which covered employment, stated that employers could not fire, refuse to hire, or deny "employment opportunities" because of an individual's race, color, sex, or national origin.[4]

In its original form, the act applied only to race and national origin. The modern women's liberation movement was still several years in the future, and equality of the sexes was even more controversial than equality of the races. During the House debate on the act, Rep. Howard Smith of Virginia, a strong opponent of any civil rights legislation, introduced an amendment banning sex discrimination. He hoped that this amendment would make the act so ridiculous that nobody would vote for it. For a while it looked as though he had succeeded; when his amendment was read to the House, many representatives actually burst out laughing.[5]

Title VII also states that if a contractor has discriminated, the federal courts have the power to "order such affirmative action as may be appropriate, which may include . . . reinstatement or hiring of employees with or without back pay . . . or any other equitable relief as the court deems appropriate." Once again there was confusion about the exact meaning of the phrase "affirmative action." During the congressional debate many questions were asked. Would the act require racial quotas? Would it lead to reverse discrimination? Hubert Humphrey, a supporter, explained to critics that Title VII did not demand preferential hiring to achieve racial balance. To emphasize his point, Humphrey offered to eat the bill, page by page, if it ever resulted in discrimination against whites. Sen. Joseph Clark, another supporter, added that "quotas are themselves discriminatory."[6] In the end, a statement was added that nothing in Title VII should be interpreted to require any employer:

to grant preferential treatment to any individual or group on account of an imbalance which may exist with respect to the total number or percentage of persons of any race, color, religion, sex, or national origin

. . . in comparison with the total number or percentage [of such people in the available work force of an area].[7]

This section directly outlawed quotas of any kind.

When questioned about enforcement, Senator Clark stated that the EEOC, which replaced Kennedy's PCEEO, would have to show that "discharge or other personnel action was because of race" before a remedy was applied. Humphrey added that the employer must have "an intent to discriminate" in order to violate Title VII.[8]

The Civil Rights Act of 1964 passed and was signed into law. It covered only private employers, but in 1972 it was amended to include labor unions, employment agencies, and job training programs.

EXECUTIVE ORDER 11246

The Civil Rights Act of 1964 was joined the next year by Executive Order 11246, issued by President Lyndon Johnson. Johnson, a Texan committed to civil rights, sponsored a program of laws to create what he called the "Great Society." One of the major goals of Johnson's Great Society was racial equality. Johnson also issued Executive Order 11375, which addressed sex discrimination. Both of these executive orders were similar to Kennedy's order, but they had a little more muscle in them. Johnson created the Office of Federal Contract Compliance Programs (OFCCP). OFCCP was supposed to solve a long-standing problem— the exact meaning of "affirmative action." To do this, OFCCP issued a set of specific guidelines for its contractors. The guidelines were revised several times. The last version, adopted in 1971, is still in effect today.[9]

The guidelines spell out exactly what an employer must

do regarding affirmative action. First of all, each company must analyze its work force. All jobs must be ranked in order of salary, and the number of minorities and women in each category must be listed. The company must also provide statistics on the number of minority people and working women in the area. (The percentage of women is always roughly 50 percent, but it is assumed that some women voluntarily choose not to work outside the home.) The company must also determine the number of women and minorities who might reasonably be promoted and analyze training programs that might benefit these groups.

When all this is done, it should be fairly clear which departments or ranks have far fewer minority or female workers than might be expected. The order assumes that a great difference is due to discrimination and then requires an affirmative action plan. Recognizing that each company is different, the order does not specify any particular program but instead allows the contractor to design its own. A feature of each plan must be "goals and timetables" for countering the effects of discrimination. According to the order, goals should be "significant, measureable, and attainable (achievable)" but not "rigid and inflexible quotas."[10] Basically, the goals and timetables are intended to make the affirmative-action plan concrete. Instead of saying, "Giant Corporation will attempt to attract more black workers," the company says, "Giant Corporation will try to recruit and train fifty minority applicants in the next eighteen months in order to fill 3 percent of its skilled craft jobs."

Executive Order 11246 therefore authorized the use of statistics to prove discrimination—something the Civil Rights Act had expressly forbidden. However, the goals required by Executive Order 11246 are not "inflexible quotas." A company that does not fulfill them will probably not be penalized. If Giant Corporation trains only three minority applicants in eighteen months, the company can still claim a good faith effort to meet its goal. The OFCCP must prove discrimination before penalties are given.

THE CONSTRUCTION INDUSTRY

Shortly after Johnson's order went into effect, it became obvious that the construction industry was going to present special problems. Executive Order 11246 covers contractors, but few construction workers are permanently employed by the same company. Carpenters, for example, belong to a union that acts as the members' employment agency. When a building site needs five carpenters for two weeks' work, the request goes to the union hiring hall. (There are nonunion construction workers, but few major companies will hire them.) Workers who are between jobs register at the hiring hall, and when work is available for them, they are sent out.

Many construction unions have had a long history of racial and sexual prejudice. In 1971, blacks accounted for less than 4 percent of the memberships in eleven out of sixteen building trades unions. In the highest-paid trades, black union memberships averaged less than 1.7 percent. A 1969 survey of construction-work unions showed that 58 percent of the local union branches had no black members at all; an additional 28 percent had less than 1 percent.[11] The record for women shows smaller numbers. In 1970, female membership in construction unions stood at 0.6 percent.[12] Furthermore, even those minority workers who managed to join a union were often discriminated against. Some unions maintained separate hiring halls and seniority lists for minority and white workers, with minorities getting less frequent and less desirable jobs.

OFCCP began a number of programs in the late 1960s

and early 1970s to correct this situation. "Hometown plans" were affirmative-action programs designed by committees in many areas around the country. The committees consisted of representatives from local civil rights, union, and business groups. By working through the unions, OFCCP was able to obtain at least partial support for integration. One hometown plan in St. Louis, Missouri, permitted minority workers with some construction experience to move through apprenticeship training more quickly than normal. Inexperienced workers were allowed to sample various trades for six months before selecting one for advanced training. All the hometown plans had goals and timetables for increasing minority work in construction.[13]

Seven cities judged to have especially severe discrimination records were put on "Philadelphia plans," a name based on one of the cities in the group. Philadelphia plans had goals and timetables set by OFCCP instead of local committees. The goals still applied to the contractors, since legally OFCCP had no power to regulate any other organization. Unions and national labor leaders had no input into Philadelphia Plans, and many were bitterly opposed to the programs. However, opponents and supporters alike were forced to accept the plans or lose work on federal projects.[14]

AFFIRMATIVE ACTION
IN THE SEVENTIES

In the late 1960s and early 1970s, most federal agencies that provide benefits to employers developed affirmative action requirements of their own. In order to qualify for government benefits, the employer had to evaluate the work force and set goals and timetables for improvement in minority and female representation. One of these agencies was the Department of Health, Education, and Welfare (HEW). HEW began to examine the number and rank of minority and female teachers around the country. The percentages in higher education were small, and as a result, many universities created affirmative action plans.

Another development was a 1977 federal law requiring that 10 percent of all construction money for certain public works be awarded to minority- or female-owned businesses. Many state and local governments passed set-aside laws in the 1970s and 1980s.

During the same decades, the number of affirmative-action plans in use around the country exploded. Companies scrambled to add affirmative action officers to their personnel departments, to design recruitment and training programs, and to identify likely minority and female candidates for promotion. In some cases this spurt of activity resulted from pangs of conscience; some companies genuinely wanted to be fair. However, in other cases the pangs were of fear. The Civil Rights Act of 1964 had authorized the courts to provide remedies—including back pay—to victims of discrimination. Charging violation of the Civil Rights Act, many minority and women workers sued their companies in the early 1970s, and many of them won.

A few hundred people asking for back pay wouldn't make much of a dent in corporations' pocketbooks. However, many of the suits were class action suits. That is, Mary Jones, who was denied a promotion because of her sex, files suit on behalf of herself and all the other women who suffered a similar injury. Upon losing, Jones's company must pay her—and perhaps thousands of colleagues—back pay and damages. This can add up fairly quickly. The communications giant AT&T, for example, was ordered by the court to make $38 million in payments to its minority and female workers in 1973.[15] General Motors was fined $42 million in a similar judgment.[16] These and other settlements convinced business leaders to take affirmative action seriously. As one personnel executive put it, "It took a while to understand what the law really meant, but those class action lawsuits proved very effective teachers. And, when the light finally dawned, we really went to work on it."[17]

As affirmative action grew, so did the controversy surrounding it. This was partly the result of the recession that hit the country in the mid-1970s. The 1960s had been a time of great prosperity. When minority groups and women asked for a larger share of the economic pie, there seemed to be enough for everyone. In the 1970s the picture was different: Unemployment jumped from 4.9 percent in 1970 to 8.5 percent in 1974, the inflation rate caused prices to double during the decade, and business profits dropped. Some whites, particularly those in entry-level or low-paying jobs, began to feel that they were victims of reverse discrimination.[18]

The controversy was also fueled by a number of widely publicized court cases. Most of them involved fixed hiring or promotion quotas given to some organizations convicted of violating the Civil Rights Act of 1964. The San Francisco Fire Department is a good example of this. In 1969 there were only four black firefighters in San Francisco, a city with a 43 percent minority population. The next year a coalition of rights organizations sued the San Francisco Civil Service Commission on behalf of "all Negro and Mexican-American San Francisco area adults fully qualified to be firemen" and "all Negro and Mexican-American San Francisco adults desirous of having their homes protected by an integrated department."[19]

The rights groups were concerned about the written test used to determine hiring. Applicants took a variety of physical tests and a written exam but were mainly ranked according to their scores on the written exam. Firefighters were hired in order of rank. The civil rights groups charged that the test was discriminatory and did not measure skills needed for firefighting. The judge agreed and ordered the city to devise a fairer test. A new exam was written, but it was very similar to the old one; the judge asked for another. Once again the exam was redone, but the court ruled that it still did not measure job performance.

Finally, in November 1973, the judge lost patience. He went back to the last written test and found 314 whites and 118 minority applicants who had passed. He ordered the fire department to choose an equal number of white and minority people until all the minority applicants were employed.[20]

In the early 1970s similar quota orders were handed down for the police and fire departments of Minneapolis, Boston, Los Angeles, Baltimore, Philadelphia, and many other cities around the country. Quotas were also imposed by the courts on US Steel, Goodyear Tire and Rubber, Detroit Edison, and other private companies, as well as many unions. In most cases these decisions were appealed to higher courts or challenged in countersuits. A number of whites who saw themselves as victims of reverse discrimination also sued.[21]

AFFIRMATIVE ACTION
IN THE REAGAN YEARS

During his first press conference as president, Ronald Reagan took aim at the affirmative action policies established by his predecessors. In his view, the civil rights program had gone too far, and the balance had begun to shift from remedies for past discrimination to reverse discrimination against whites. He pledged to change several aspects of affirmative action, beginning with quotas for minority and female employment. As he explained to reporters, "I'm old enough to remember when quotas existed in the United States for the purpose of discrimination, and I don't want to see that happen again."[22]

In Reagan's view, any numerical requirement for hiring is a quota, not just the mandatory amounts prescribed by the courts in Civil Rights Act lawsuits. This includes the goals and timetables required by Johnson's Executive Order 11246. In August 1985, Reagan officials wrote a draft of a new executive order to replace 11246. The draft was for Reagan's consideration; it would have no legal force until the president signed it. The draft revoked all the regulations that required numerical goals and the use of statistics to prove discrimination. It also added:

Nothing in this executive order shall be interpreted to require or provide a legal basis for a government contractor or subcontractor to utilize any numerical quota, goal, or ratio, or otherwise to discriminate against, or grant any preference to, any individual or group on the basis of race, color, religion, sex, or national origin. . . .[23]

These words would not actually make goals and timetables illegal, but they would weaken affirmative action plans considerably. When sued by white employees for reverse discrimination, many employers defend themselves by claiming they are only following federal regulations. If the federal regulations were changed, this defense would no longer be usable.

The draft order caused a storm of protest, especially from civil rights groups. Barry Goldstein, assistant counsel for the NAACP's Legal Defense and Education Fund, said that "the draft order . . . removes one of the most critical forms of evidence to prove the existence of discrimination."[24] Congress also protested: Seventy senators and 200 representatives signed a letter against the proposed executive order.[25] Surprisingly, business executives were also disturbed by the proposed changes. William McEwen of the National Association of Manufacturers (which had voted an endorsement of affirmative action earlier in the year) said that if the draft were signed, "progress towards equal opportunity would be eminently slower."[26] However, the draft order was applauded by many conservative political groups and others who oppose affirmative action.

Reagan never signed the draft order, but his administration did undertake a number of other policies with important effects on affirmative action. In the early 1980s, the Justice Department and the EEOC concentrated on individual suits instead of class actions because in Reagan's view only the actual victim of discrimination is entitled to a remedy. The EEOC also moved to change the standards used to evaluate job testing. Under previous administrations, if a job test excluded most minority and female applicants, it was up to the employer to prove that the test was a fair measure of the actual skills needed for the job. In the mid-1980s the EEOC proposed a policy which assumed that any exam prepared by testing experts was acceptable even if it resulted in higher scores for white males.[27]

The Justice Department also changed its policy toward civil rights in the Reagan years. After a Supreme Court decision outlawing quotas in layoffs, Atty. Gen. Edwin Meese claimed that the court had judged all quotas illegal. He wrote to fifty groups around the country that had court-ordered affirmative action settlements. The Justice Department wanted any settlements that included quotas dropped. The Supreme Court later ruled that quotas in hiring and promotions were permissible under certain circumstances. Yet even before that ruling, most of the Justice Department letters were ignored. The attitude seemed to be "It's working; leave it alone." Several people who received letters complained that the quotas had resulted from suits brought by the Justice Department during previous administrations. As Mayor E. P. Larkins of Pompano Beach, Florida, said about affirmative action in his community, "We don't need the Department of Justice tampering with something mandated (ordered) by the Department of Justice."[28]

According to critics, affirmative action also slowed during the 1980s because the Reagan administration didn't enforce the laws vigorously. During previous administrations twenty-six federal contractors were barred from doing business with the government because of violations of Executive Order 11246. During the Reagan years the numbers dropped to two.[29] The proportion of civil rights cases filed by the Justice Department also decreased—from 5.4 percent of all suits in Carter's last year as president to 1.9 percent in Reagan's first year.[30]

As the new administration takes office in 1989, affirmative action policies will undoubtedly be reviewed. The views of the new president and his team of officials will shape law enforcement and Justice Department prosecutions—and affirmative action—for some time to come.

4

AFFIRMATIVE
ACTION IN
THE COURTS

One-third of the power of our country's federal government resides in nine black-robed figures—the justices of the U.S. Supreme Court. Appointed for life by the president and confirmed by the Senate, the justices are the court of last resort. Most of the cases they hear (including all of the affirmative-action cases discussed in this chapter) were heard several times by lower courts. Once the case reaches the Supreme Court, however, all appeals are exhausted. The justices' verdict is final and may be appealed nowhere else.

One of their most important functions is to interpret the U.S. Constitution. While the framers of the document could never have envisioned our complex modern world, they did declare general principles that may be applied to any society. If the court hears a case involving a law that violates those principles, it can declare the law unconstitutional. Any arrests or orders that have been made because of that law are then invalid.

Supreme Court decisions are accompanied by written explanations, or opinions, which describe the reasoning of the court and other cases or laws relevant to the issue. The justices voting on the winning side publish a majority opinion, and the justices who disagree file a dissenting opinion, explaining why they believe the majority is wrong. Several justices may sign one opinion, but all justices have the right to file separate opinions if they feel the majority or dissenting opinions do not completely explain their own beliefs. These opinions, as well as the final vote, are used as guidelines by lower courts all around the country.

The opinions accompanying the court's decisions on affirmative action are often perplexing. One magazine writer referred to them as pieces of a puzzle that no one, including the court itself, knows how to solve completely. This confusion is probably the result of great disagreement among the nine justices. Many of the cases involving affirmative action have been decided by very close votes—five to four or six to three. Justices have even voted with the majority on some points and with the minority on others. Even when the justices vote alike, their separate opinions often explain that they did so for entirely different reasons!

GRIGGS v. DUKE POWER COMPANY

The *Brown* v. *the Board of Education* decision described in chapter 2 outlawed some official policies of racial discrimination. *Griggs* v. *Duke Power Company,* a 1971 case, tackled subtler forms of prejudice.

For years the Duke Power Company of North Carolina had had a system: All blacks were assigned to the labor department, while most whites were sent to the company's other divisions. The separation of races was reflected in the paychecks: The highest salaries in labor were lower than the lowest salaries in the other departments.

After the Civil Rights Act was passed in 1964, the job discrimination at Duke Power Company was challenged. The company then created a new rule. Anyone who applied for a job outside the labor department had to be a high school graduate and pass two tests. Current employees of the other divisions (all whites) could keep their jobs and be promoted without these requirements. Since all the blacks were in the labor department, none could be promoted without following the new rules. This was a significant barrier. In the early 1960s, only about 12 percent of black males (and 34 percent of white males) in North Carolina had finished high school.

Black workers charged that the company's requirements had nothing to do with job performance. After all, many employees were being kept on and even given better positions without this achievement. The real purpose, they claimed, was to keep blacks in their place—at the bottom of the ladder. The Supreme Court unanimously agreed. Chief Justice Warren Burger referred in his opinion to Aesop's fable of the fox and the stork. In this fable, the fox invited the stork to supper, only to present him with food in a shallow dish. The stork's long bill couldn't draw food from such a container, and as the fox dined, the stork looked on helplessly. According to Burger, the seemingly free opportunity for blacks to advance at Duke was like the stork's dinner invitation—a sham. Burger added:

> Practices, procedures, or tests neutral on their face, and even neutral in terms of intent, cannot be maintained if they operate to 'freeze' [previous] discriminatory employment practices. . . . If an employment practice which operates to exclude Negroes cannot be shown to be related to job performance, the practice is prohibited.

The Griggs decision was important for future affirmative action cases in several ways. First of all, it forced employers to examine their hiring and promotion processes and to eliminate the effects of prejudice. Second, it established the fact that prejudice may be subtle. In effect, it told employers, "Don't just seem fair—be fair."

However, the opinion also stated that the law "does not command that any person be hired simply because he was formerly the subject of discrimination, or because he is a member of a minority group." This seems to rule out most affirmative action programs. Nevertheless, those programs flourished in the decade after Griggs.[1]

THE REGENTS OF THE UNIVERSITY OF CALIFORNIA v. ALLAN BAKKE

On October 12, 1977, there were a number of long lines for tickets. Some were composed of baseball fans hoping to see a World Series game between the New York Yankees and the Los Angeles Dodgers. Another line snaked up the stone steps of the Supreme Court. The court was scheduled to hear case number 76-811. Proponents and opponents of affirmative action waited patiently to hear arguments about whether a white male, Allan Bakke, should be admitted to the University of California Medical School at Davis.

The case had begun more than six years earlier when Bakke, an engineer for NASA, decided to become a doctor. Bakke had graduated near the top of his class at the University of Minnesota. He served in the Vietnam War and then began his post with the space program. To prepare for his medical career, Bakke had taken extra courses in biology and chemistry and volunteered as an aide in a hospital

Demonstrators for affirmative action in Detroit

• 68

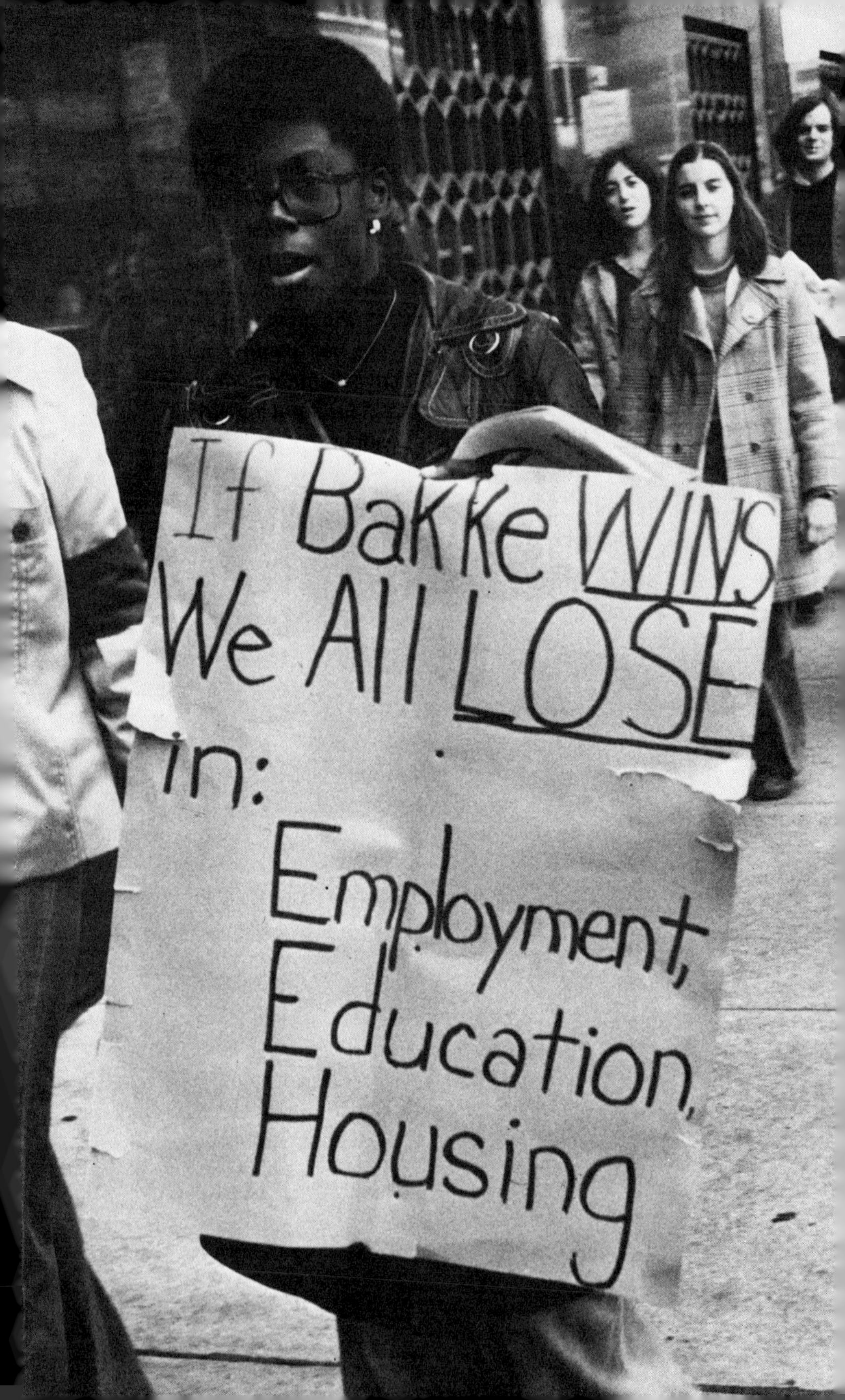
If Bakke WINS
We All LOSE
in:
Employment,
Education,
Housing

emergency room, all while holding down a full-time job. Clearly, he was a hardworking, determined man.

However, Allan Bakke had problems. One of those problems faces everyone who applies to medical school: There are far more qualified applicants than available places for students. Another was peculiar to Allan Bakke: at thirty-three, he was a decade older than the average applicant. According to Bakke, he also had a third problem—his race.

Several medical schools rejected Bakke immediately, citing his age. The University of California at Davis invited him in for an interview. On the Davis application an item read, "Applicants from economically and educationally disadvantaged backgrounds are evaluated by a special subcommittee of the admission committee. If you wish your application to be considered by this group, check this space." Applicants who marked this item were considered by a special task force. The task force had been created in 1969 to help bring more minority and economically disadvantaged students into the school. Students applying for task-force consideration could be of any race. However, in practice no whites had ever been admitted through this special procedure, and few minorities had entered Davis through the regular channels.

The task force was allotted 16 out of the school's 100 openings; another 5 were given to the dean of the school. The dean's places often went to applicants with good connections, such as relatives with powerful jobs in the medical establishment. Students who did not check the task-force box and who were not referred by the dean were evaluated by the regular admissions committee.

Allan Bakke fared well during his interview, but he was still rejected by the school. He applied again, was rejected again, and then sued the school, claiming that he had been discriminated against because of his race. Bakke believed that some task-force students were less qualified than he and had been admitted instead of him solely because they were members of minority groups. Bakke based his claim on the fact that the average scores of task-force students were lower than the average scores of other students at Davis and lower than Bakke's own scores. (However, the range of scores overlapped. Some task-force students scored higher than Bakke, and some students accepted under the normal admissions program scored lower than Bakke.)

The university countered Bakke's arguments by explaining that all the students at Davis were fully qualified. Because of society's past discrimination, the university claimed that it was justified in considering race as one of the factors in the admissions process. According to the university, the task force also met two important goals: It created a more diverse student body, which enhanced the students' education, and it trained doctors who were more likely to serve disadvantaged communities after graduation.

The case worked its way through the lower courts; Allan Bakke won each time, and each time the university appealed. By the time it reached the Supreme Court, *The Regents of the University of California* v. *Allan Bakke* had attracted national attention. One hundred sixty organizations filed briefs—written arguments for the court to consider—for or against Bakke's case.

The court announced its decision in June 1978. Four justices voted to admit Allan Bakke to medical school. They believed that the task-force program had discriminated against Bakke on the basis of race. Another four voted the opposite. In their view, the Davis admissions program was constitutional and Bakke's rights had not been violated. Justice Lewis Powell broke the deadlock, so his opinion became the verdict of the court. He agreed that Bakke should be admitted to Davis because the admissions procedure

was unfair, but he did not totally rule out the possibility of affirmative action programs. Powell said these programs could not assign a particular number of places to minority candidates, as the Davis program did. However, they could rate race or ethnic background as a positive factor in their consideration of applicants.

When the ruling was announced, both sides claimed victory. Opponents of affirmative action saw it as a victory for the white majority. Supporters celebrated the fact that affirmative action could be constitutional. As for Allan Bakke, he entered medical school on September 25, 1978.[2]

UNITED STEELWORKERS OF AMERICA v. BRIAN E. WEBER

A year almost to the day after its decision in the Bakke case, the Supreme Court ruled in the case of *United Steelworkers of America* v. *Brian E. Weber.* Weber was a white laboratory technician at the Kaiser Aluminum plant in Gramercy, Louisiana. That part of Louisiana is 43 percent black; nevertheless, in the 1970s only 5 of the 290 skilled craftworkers at the plant were members of minority groups. The United Steelworkers Union, which represents Kaiser employees, negotiated an agreement with the company to increase the number of minorities in higher-paying positions. Kaiser created two separate seniority lists—one black and one white.

Allan Bakke arrives at the
University of California
at Davis for his first day of
classes following the Supreme
Court's ruling in his favor.

• 73

The same number of candidates for an on-the-job training program were to be selected from each list until the percentage of minority workers in skilled jobs equaled the proportion of minorities living in the surrounding area.

Brian Weber applied for the general-repairman training program; he knew that this position carried a higher salary and more job security. He sued when he was turned down, claiming that black employees with less seniority than he had been chosen for extra training.

The Supreme Court ruled that Weber's rights had not been violated and that Kaiser's affirmative action program was legal. The court pointed out that the union representing all the workers had voluntarily negotiated this solution in order to make up for past discrimination. No white worker had been fired and replaced by a black, and white workers could still be promoted when there were openings. For these reasons, the court believed that Kaiser was treating all its workers fairly.[3]

FULLILOVE v. KLUTZNIK

The Fullilove case was a challenge to the Public Works Employment Act of 1977. That act distributed funds to state and local governments for use on projects such as roads, bridges, hospitals, etc. According to the act, 10 percent of the money each government received was to be set aside to obtain services or supplies from businesses owned by minorities. The act defined "minority" as black, Hispanic, Oriental, Indian, Eskimo, and Aleut. This type of set-aside has often been created by local governments for their own areas, but the Public Works Employment Act was a national program.

The act was challenged before the Supreme Court, which ruled it constitutional in 1980. Chief Justice Warren Burger stated in the majority opinion that " 'a sharing of the burden' by otherwise innocent parties is [permissible]." That is, the white business community might lose money because of this act. Nevertheless, that was fair since for so many years that community had enjoyed an advantage over minority business owners.

Justice Stevens dissented vehemently. If the government is to use these racial classifications, he said, it will have to study Nazi Germany's classification methods for determining who is or is not a Jew. Otherwise, how will we know who qualifies as minority? Such categories, Stevens believed, are contrary to the real goal of America—a color-blind society.[4]

FIREFIGHTERS LOCAL UNION #1784
v. CARL W. STOTTS

Lots of little kids say they want to be firemen when they grow up. In Memphis, Tennessee, that ambition was once limited mainly to whites. In the early 1970s, only 4 percent of the city's firefighters were black, even though blacks make up 35 percent of the local population. In 1980 the Memphis city government was sued for racial discrimination. One of the men bringing suit was Carl W. Stotts, a black firefighter. Before the case went to trial, the city signed a consent decree—a legal agreement approved by the court—to institute an affirmative action program. Fifty percent of all firefighters hired were to be members of minority groups. The plan would be in effect until the number of black firefighters was in proportion to the number of minority people in the area.

By 1981 the Memphis Fire Department had hired eighteen minority firefighters, and 11.5 percent of the department was now black. Then the city announced budget cuts;

twenty-four firefighters would have to be laid off. If the layoffs were done strictly by seniority, fifteen of those blacks would be fired. The court amended the consent decree so that three blacks and twenty-one whites would lose their jobs. The whites who had been laid off sued, charging that their seniority system had been violated because of race.

The case, *Firefighters Local Union #1784* v. *Carl W. Stotts,* reached the Supreme Court in 1984. The court, voting six to three, ruled in favor of the white firefighters. Justice Byron White wrote in the majority opinion that "it is inappropriate to deny any innocent employee the benefits of his seniority in order to prescribe a remedy in a pattern or practice [of discrimination] suit." Key factors cited by the court were that racial discrimination in the fire department had never been proved, white employees had been directly harmed, and the original consent decree had been changed by the court.

In an unusual move, Justice White added an extra comment on affirmative action. Remedies for racial prejudice, he said, should be applied only to actual victims. It was not enough to belong to a group that had suffered discrimination. Justice Stevens signed this opinion but added that the extra comment was only a statement of belief and was not legally binding.[5]

WYGANT v. SCHOOL BOARD
OF JACKSON, MICHIGAN

The Stotts case made it clear that the court could not order layoffs as part of an affirmative action plan. But could this type of affirmative action be done voluntarily? That question came up in 1984 in the case of *Wygant* v. *School Board of Jackson, Michigan.*

Most people would agree that children benefit from good role models—adults who teach not algebra or grammar but life, simply by living it themselves. The school board of Jackson, Michigan, wanted its integrated student body to study with teachers of all races. It was particularly concerned that minority students be in contact with teachers of their own race. The problem was that the faculty of the Jackson district had once been almost totally white. The board made an effort to integrate its staff; however, a large proportion of the newest teachers were members of minority groups. That meant that in the usual "last hired, first fired" system, any reduction in faculty would fall most heavily on minority teachers. The school board therefore negotiated a special contract: In the event of layoffs, three whites would be dismissed for every black teacher fired.

In 1981 fewer children enrolled in school, and a number of teachers were laid off. Wendy Wygant, a white kindergarten teacher, was one of them. She joined several colleagues in a suit against the school board, claiming that race should not be a factor in deciding who is to lose a job.

The Supreme Court agreed, voting five to four that the Jackson School District plan violated the white teachers' civil rights. According to Justice Powell, who wrote the opinion for the majority, affirmative action in hiring and layoffs are very different. Powell explained that in making up for past discrimination, "it may be necessary to take race into account" and "innocent persons may be called upon to bear some of the burden of the remedy." Powell added that in hiring, the burden is spread throughout society generally. Firing is a much greater disruption in an innocent person's life and should not be imposed on account of race. Furthermore, there was no proof that the Jackson board had discriminated in the past, and the general idea of discrimination by society was not enough to justify "financial as well as psychological effects" on whites who were perfectly innocent.[6]

SHEET METAL

New York City Local 28 of the Sheet Metal Workers Union had been in and out of court many times between 1963 and 1986. The charge was discrimination; just about every union sheet-metal worker in New York was white, and the courts agreed that this was due to racial prejudice. After each court appearance the judges directed the union to admit non-white workers. Each time the union delayed; twice it was held in contempt for not obeying court orders. By the early 1980s the union's files looked like alphabet soup: an Affirmative Action Plan Order (AAPO) was replaced by a Revised Affirmative Action Plan Order (RAAPO) which gave way to an Amended Affirmative Action Plan Order (AAAPO).

In 1983 the court lost patience. The union was to be composed of 29.23 percent minority workers by August 1987—no ifs, ands, or buts about it. The union appealed, taking the case as far as the Supreme Court. It argued that affirmative action was "corruption of blood," punishment of children for their parents' offenses. Corruption of blood is specifically prohibited by Article III of the Constitution. The union's past discrimination, the workers argued, was no reason to impose racial quotas on the present system. The union added that "the race conscious program . . . provides benefits to non-whites causing discrimination against whites."

The Supreme Court upheld the affirmative action order. Although in the Bakke case the court had balked at a specific quota, the justices ruled in 1986 that "goals and timetables" were permissible because of the union's previous defiance of court orders and its long history of discrimination.[7]

THE CLEVELAND VANGUARDS

The Supreme Court ruled on another "quota" dispute the same day it decided the Sheet Metal case. The Vanguards, an association of minority firefighters in Cleveland, Ohio, charged the city with discrimination in hiring, assigning, and promoting firefighters. The group negotiated a special agreement whereby half of all promotions would go to minority workers until an adequate proportion of high-ranking minorities was reached. Local 93 of the International Association of Firefighters, which represents the Cleveland workers and is predominantly white, challenged the plan. The court ruled that the affirmative action plan was acceptable because it met certain standards. It was designed to erase the effects of past discrimination, it did not necessarily damage white workers, and it was to be dropped after certain goals were met. According to the court, this is a "narrowly tailored" solution—one that fits the problem but does not go beyond what is essential for relief.

In both the Sheet Metal and the Vanguard cases, the court also ruled on another important point. Contradicting Justice White's comment in the Stott case, the court officially held that if an employer had discrimination against blacks and Hispanics as a group, affirmative action could also be directed to the group, not just to the particular people whose careers had been harmed because of prejudice.[8]

UNITED STATES v. PARADISE

Like "a hand in a glove." That's the phrase the Justice Department used in 1987 when it brought the case of the

Alabama state troopers to the U.S. Supreme Court. The Justice Department argued that affirmative action remedies were permissible only if they fit the problem as closely as a glove fits a hand. According to the Justice Department, Alabama's plan for its police officers was more like a loose mitten.

The roots of the case stretch back into Alabama's history. Like much of the South, Alabama had discriminatory laws. With the pressure of the civil rights movement, many of those laws were taken off the books. However, while legalized segregation ended, traditional segregation remained. This was evident in many areas, particularly in the state police force. In 1963 the force was used to block school integration in the city of Tuskegee. In 1965 television viewers saw troopers hitting black demonstrators participating in a "freedom march." As late as 1972 not one Alabama state trooper was black.

In that year a federal court ordered the force to integrate. By the mid-1980s, 27 percent of the state's troopers were black. However, no black ranked higher than sergeant. Civil rights advocates charged that racism was preventing blacks from rising to higher positions. The lower courts agreed and approved a complicated plan in which half of all promotions would go to minority troopers, provided qualified candidates were available, until 25 percent of the upper ranks were filled by non-white officers.

The Justice Department, which firmly opposed affirmative action during the Reagan years, brought suit to block the plan. Solicitor General Charles Fried told the Supreme Court that the one-for-one quota was "excessive" and "profoundly illegal." The Supreme Court, by a vote of five to four, disagreed. Justice William Brennan wrote the majority opinion in which he stated that the long-standing, stubborn racism of the Alabama State Police Department justified "race-conscious relief." Brennan added his belief that whites were not unnecessarily penalized by the plan since it only "postponed the promotions of qualified whites." Justice John Paul Stevens, in a separate opinion, added that in cases of proven discrimination courts have "broad and flexible authority to remedy the wrongs." Sandra Day O'Connor wrote the dissent, stating that the lower court should have explored other remedies, such as fines, before turning to a quota.[9]

JOHNSON v. TRANSPORTATION AGENCY

"It's not a job for a woman." That's what one of Diane Joyce's co-workers said when she was promoted to road dispatcher for the Santa Clara County Transportation Agency in 1980. Joyce was used to hearing comments like that. Four years before, she had become the first woman to work on a road crew, shoveling asphalt, patching holes, and doing other heavy work. When she heard about the job as dispatcher (a desk job with a higher salary), she was eager to apply.

The transportation agency had begun a voluntary affirmative action plan in 1978. The program did not call for specific numbers of women in each job; it noted that there might not be a large number of women with the proper qualifications interested in some of the positions. Instead, the plan called for a sincere effort to find and promote qualified women into the traditionally male, better-paying positions. By 1980, when Diane Joyce applied for the dispatcher job, not one of the agency's positions of that rank was held by a female. In fact, women were still clustered in traditionally female positions of secretary and clerk.

Seven applicants qualified for the dispatcher job; Diane Joyce was one, and Paul Johnson was another. The local superintendent picked Johnson, who had been rated 75 on his interview. The county affirmative action coordinator recommended Joyce, who had received a 73. When Joyce got the job, Johnson sued.

After a number of lower court battles, the Supreme Court upheld Joyce's promotion by a vote of six to three. Justice Brennan praised the county's affirmative action plan as "moderate" and "flexible" and noted that it was temporary and would be dropped when its goals were met. According to Brennan, Joyce was not promoted because she was a woman. She was qualified for the position, and the affirmative action plan simply considered her sex as one factor in her favor. This was justified because of "the obvious imbalance in the skilled craft division."[10]

The Johnson decision was historic in a number of ways. It was the first time that an affirmative action case involving sex had come before the court; all the previous cases had dealt with race. Also, the court had ruled clearly that statistics (such as 238 men and no women) could be used to establish the need for affirmative action. Lastly, the majority opinion allowed employers to establish affirmative action plans voluntarily without admitting to previous racism or sexism. Before the Johnson case, an employer with an affirmative action plan could be sued by women or minorities for back pay and other benefits if the employer admitted to discrimination. Without this admission, the employer could be sued by white males for reverse discrimination. As the *New York Times* put it, the decision allowed an employer "to do good without first having to look bad."[11]

LOWER COURT DECISIONS

Lower state and federal courts have also ruled on affirmative action plans. As with the Supreme Court cases, the verdicts are often confusing or even contradictory. Furthermore, when a new Supreme Court decision is issued, lower court rulings must often be changed in order to comply with the judgment of the nation's highest court. Here are a few important lower court cases:

- *Ethridge* v. *Rhodes.* A federal court ruled in 1967 that employers must show an integrated work force before bidding for public contracts.[12]

- *Contractors of Eastern Pennsylvania* v. *United States.* In response to a challenge to the Philadelphia plans, a federal district court ruled that the president did have the authority to issue Executive Order 11246 and that the Philadelphia plans were legal.[13]

- *Communications Workers of America* v. *Equal Employment Opportunity Commission.* The giant American Telephone and Telegraph Company signed a consent decree in 1973 to end job bias against women and minorities. Part of the decree provided for "goals and timetables" for hiring and promoting minorities and women. In 1977, the union sued both AT&T and the government in order to overturn the consent decree. The court upheld the decree, stating that the goals and timetables were permissible because of past discrimination.[14]

- *Firestone Tire and Rubber Company* v. *Marshall.* In 1981, the Texas District Court ruled that a difference in percentage between the number of minorities or women in the labor force and the number employed by the company did not have to be exactly the same. In other words, the court held that statistics alone do not prove discrimination.[15]

- *Setser* v. *Novack Investment Company.* In 1981, the court ruled that in order to justify affirmative action, the employer must show that discrimination existed. However, the court said that this could be shown in many ways, including the employer's own statistics about the work force.[16]

• *Berkman* v. *City of New York.* In 1982, a federal court ruled that the New York City Fire Department must change its test for applicants. According to the court, the previous test discriminated against women and did not really measure job performance. In 1987, the appeals court overturned this ruling and reinstated the old test.[17]

• Firefighters of Washington, D.C. A 1987 federal appeals court decision struck down a plan in Washington, D.C., that called for a 60 percent quota for blacks in hiring. The court stated that preference for minorities in hiring is illegal unless justified by evidence of past or present discrimination.[18]

The split votes on many Supreme Court cases and the disagreement among lower courts mean that the issue of affirmative action will be sensitive to changes in court personnel. As new judges take office, their views will help determine the legality of affirmative action plans. This is particularly true of the Supreme Court. Currently, several of the judges are over eighty years old and in poor health, so vacancies are likely in the next few years.

One vacancy has already occurred. In 1987, Justice Lewis Powell retired. Before Justice Anthony Kennedy took his place in early 1988, one affirmative action case, *Marino* v. *Ortiz,* was heard by the court. A group of white New York City police officers had sued to overturn a plan whereby the number of black and Hispanic police officers promoted to sergeant would be increased. The plan called for the promotion of some minority officers whose test scores would not normally qualify them for the rank of sergeant. The lower courts had turned down the whites' suit, saying that the white officers had not used the proper procedure for challenging the plan.

The court vote was four to four, and as in all ties, the judgment of the lower court was allowed to stand. Clearly the affirmative action decisions of the divided Supreme Court will be influenced by Kennedy's future votes.[19]

What will those votes be? No one really knows, since Justice Kennedy never had the opportunity to rule on affirmative action during his career as a lower court judge. The justice did say during his confirmation hearings that his experience as a law professor "taught me the arguments in favor of affirmative action. . . . I know of no professor of legal education that does not think it is highly important that we have a representative group of black law students in the law schools." However, Kennedy added, "I recognize that . . . there are different kinds of programs that may represent constitutional questions."[20]

5

THE CASE FOR AFFIRMATIVE ACTION

It's just about time for the race to begin, and the runners are flexing muscles, reviewing strategy, and preparing for the ordeal ahead. At last, everyone is in position, and a split second later the starter's pistol goes off.

But something's wrong! That black man in lane nine—his foot is caught in the starting block. And someone in the crowd is holding the arm of the woman next to him. Over there, that fellow from Puerto Rico, there's a barrier across his lane. The young Chicano, those black women—they're all caught. They can't begin!

As they struggle to free themselves, the unlucky runners watch their rivals zoom around the track. One lap, two, three . . . Finally all obstacles are out of the way, and the minority and female runners streak down the track, staring helplessly at the white male front-runners, now miles in the lead.

Supporters of affirmative action believe American history is something like this race. After centuries of prejudice and discriminatory laws, a number of civil rights measures were passed in the 1960s and 1970s. Yet minority and female runners, freed suddenly of restraint and legally equal, could not possibly catch up with white males in the economic "race." The favored "runners" had enjoyed advantages—inherited wealth, better education, opportunity for employment—built up over centuries. To simply say that jobs, promotions, and contracts belong to those who merit them is as unjust, supporters claim, as it would be unjust to award medals to race winners who had begun running long before the other entrants. According to supporters, affirmative action is not a gift to minorities and women or a punishment for white males. Instead, it is simply a way of evening up the starting point of the race.

Affirmative action supporters also charge that the merit ideal has never really been consistently applied in America. Apart from outright discrimination, other factors have always been involved in hiring and education. Civil service exams routinely award extra points to veterans, and seniority is often the major factor in layoffs and promotions—not talent. A typical college application asks if the student is the son or daughter of a graduate, and extra consideration is often given to applicants with such ties. Colleges also look more favorably on those with athletic talent or those from parts of the country that are not well represented in the student body.

Many informal favors are also part of the "old-boy network." An executive has lunch with a colleague and mentions that his son is just starting out in business. Can you throw some work his way? Have you got a summer job for my nephew? How about that new program at the university? Can you call your friend and get my daughter in? In this way, people with connections to those with a share of wealth and power pass on their advantages to friends and relatives.

This is such an accepted practice that it is often overlooked. The Bakke case is an example of this. While sixteen places in the medical school were assigned to the task force, five were given to the dean. Applicants with "connections" were sometimes given one of the five dean's places even if their scores were lower than those of rejected applicants. This procedure was not even mentioned during the Bakke trial, and even those who argued strongly for admission of only the best-qualified did not object to the dean's places at that time. Later, this system was eliminated at Davis, although similar procedures still exist at many other institutions.

Affirmative action, supporters claim, simply evens the odds for minorities and women. It gives the traditionally powerless the edge that many others have enjoyed in hiring, promotions, and school programs.

LOWER QUALITY?

Two men and a woman are arguing loudly on a street corner. A few shoves are exchanged, and things seem to be heating up. A crowd quickly gathers, and someone calls the police. Consider the police officers who arrive. What skills do they need to deal with this situation effectively? Intelligence—to understand how the law applies here. Judgment—to handle the growing crowd. Understanding of human nature—to identify the conflict and perhaps defuse the argument before it becomes violent. Strength—to separate the angry combatants without using firearms.

How can any test measure all these qualities? This is the question pro-affirmative action people ask. The answer they give, of course, is that no test could possibly be adequate. They feel that there are simply too many subtle qualities in the personality of a good police officer—and in the character of many other workers as well. That's why supporters do not object when scores are ignored. Often, they believe, the tests rely too heavily on one skill and exclude many better-qualified people.

Another factor supporters mention is that no affirmative action regulation requires an employer or a school to accept people who are not qualified. The law simply calls for a good-faith effort. Furthermore, for most positions there are far more satisfactory applicants than can reasonably be accommodated. Personnel or admissions officers must often choose among many excellent people. At some extremely popular universities, for example, twice as many straight-A students may apply as there are places in the freshman class. Affirmative action allows race or sex to be an additional positive point where minorities and women are proportionally underrepresented. However, it doesn't ask any school or business to make race or sex the only basis for accepting an applicant.

Affirmative action supporters also point out that workers with a variety of backgrounds are likely to contribute to the job in different ways. Instead of lowering quality, they feel, diversity strengthens the work force. Detroit's police force, for example, was once predominantly white. Yet in the early 1970s about half of all Detroit residents were black. Police violence, particularly in a special anticrime decoy unit that killed sixteen blacks in 1973, was a tense issue. Peter Sherwood, a lawyer for the NAACP, said, "Most black people thought that the police were more dangerous than the criminals. Relations were that poor."[1] A voluntary affirmative action plan raised the number of blacks in the force to 32 percent, and the attitude of Detroit's minority community toward the police became more favorable. "There's no question that affirmative action in the police department has made a dramatic difference in police-community relations here in Detroit," commented a press secretary to Mayor Coleman Young.[2]

Diversity is also important in education, according to supporters of affirmative action. They claim that just as male grammar school teachers enrich their students' education in a way that an all-female faculty could not, female college professors also give their students a different perspective. The American Association of University Professors supports this view. It issued a statement calling for "race or sex sensitive" selections because variety is "necessary for excellence."[3]

Affirmative action supporters do not believe that the goal is female doctors for female patients, Hispanic lawyers for Hispanic clients, or anything like this. However, pro-affirmative action people do believe that it is important for all groups to have representatives in the professions. Some feminists claim that female police officers might be more sensitive to women's experiences and thus deal with sex crimes more effectively. Similarly, minority doctors might be better equipped to understand the concerns of their minority patients. As the Association of American Law Schools put it, "A white student from a good undergraduate school . . . funded by a well-to-do family, views law and society differently from the way a black student would. . . . Law schools serve as the source of training of (a group of lawyers) which must satisfy the legal needs of a (mixed) society."[4] Furthermore, supporters also point out that psychologists have long recognized the importance of role models for children. Youngsters form their own identities partly from observations of adult life. If children see members of their own race and gender limited to jobs requiring a low level of skill, they may unconsciously accept only that vision of their own future. In the same way, a minority or female executive also sends a hidden message to children: This is possible for all.

In the opinion of some executives, affirmative action may also be good for business. A division manager of AT&T

commented, "Why would someone want to be a customer of an all white, male company?"[5] Others feel that increasing the number of potential applicants for work actually increases quality. It is simply better to choose from 200 male and female, white and nonwhite applicants, they say, than from 100 white males. As the chief executive officer of one company said, "One way to get ahead of our competition is to use that pool of talented women that others are overlooking."[6] A firefighter explained that after affirmative action was put into place, "We have upgraded all our standards."[7] Still another executive put it in terms of dollars and cents: "If you're excluding people who have something to contribute to your success, that's another cost item."[8]

Although everyone grumbles about the paperwork, some supporters also believe that an affirmative action analysis of the workplace is valuable. For the first time, some companies realize exactly who does what during the work day and what skills are needed to ensure a good job. In one company, for example, the affirmative action officer discovered that secretarial applicants were required to take dictation at 120 words per minute. Yet no secretary actually on the job could remember ever using stenography; all the bosses simply gave drafts of their letters or explained what was needed and let the secretaries handle the writing. The company, in effect, had been requiring and paying for a skill it did not need.[9] Supporters claim that by setting realistic standards, one may choose from the largest possible pool of applicants and improve the overall quality of the work force.

IS AFFIRMATIVE ACTION NEEDED?

Supreme Court Justice Thurgood Marshall, a black man at the very top of his profession, once stated, "It is unnecessary in 20th century America to have individual Negroes demonstrate that they have been victims of racial discrimination; the racism of our society is so pervasive that none, regardless of wealth or position, has managed to escape its impact."[10] In the opinion of Marshall and other supporters of affirmative action, minorities and women in the United States were the victims of prejudice as a group, and only a remedy that applies to the whole group is fair. Furthermore, supporters claim, individual lawsuits are time-consuming, expensive, and inconvenient. Since victims of discrimination are often the poorest, they may not be able to afford the best legal help to make their claims. Supporters see affirmative action as a powerful tool for social change on a large scale. Quite simply, they say, nothing in America is going to change for minorities and women without it.

Supporters also point out that not all discrimination is easy to prove. Human intentions can be readily hidden. "You're not our type." "We've chosen another candidate." "You're not right for the job." Who can tell when these statements are a cover-up for racism or sexism and when they are based on unbiased judgment? Employers themselves may not even be aware of their own prejudices. As David Lawrence, the publisher of the *Detroit Free Press,* said, "People perpetuate people like themselves."[11] That is, white men may be more comfortable with other white men and unconsciously choose the applicants who are most like themselves or who fit into traditional ideas. This is evident in the results of a 1987 survey: Fifty-two percent of businesses owned by white males had only white employees. Half of all minority-owned businesses had work forces that were 75 percent minority, and female-owned companies hired more women than did any other type of business.[12]

Similar trends are evident in education. A statement by the American Association of University Professors calls for

affirmative action to be sure that universities do not acci-
dentally ignore candidates because of "untested (assump-
tions) which operate to exclude women and minorities."[13]
Supporters feel that affirmative action makes everyone
more aware and puts pressure on personnel and admissions
officers to discard old stereotypes.

DOES AFFIRMATIVE ACTION WORK?

Supporters also maintain that affirmative action has made a
difference. They cite as evidence an OFCCP study done in
1983 that surveyed over seventy-seven thousand businesses. The study showed that the percentage of women
and minorities hired and promoted in key jobs increased
more in affirmative action companies than it did in un-
regulated businesses. Federal contractors registered an 18.7
percent gain for women and 23.7 percent for minorities.
Non-federal contractors, who are not subject to affirmative
action, showed only a 10.5 percent gain for women and
21.5 percent for minorities. The researchers also found that
women and minorities in affirmative action firms had
higher-level jobs than those in other companies.[14]

AT&T is an example. In 1969, before the company signed
an affirmative action agreement, 6.7 percent of all AT&T
workers were black. The percentage of the company's black
and white workers in higher-paying jobs was as follows:

	Black (percent)	White (percent)
Management	2.4	12
Skilled craft	7.2	26
Professionals	less than 1	8

In 1979, after an affirmative action plan had been in place for a short period, the percentages were very different; 14.4 percent of blacks were in management, 18.9 percent were in crafts, and 23.3 percent were professionals.[15]

Many business executives also freely admit that the changes they have made in their hiring and promotion policies are largely because of government pressure. One researcher asked 265 corporations about their programs for women. The corporations listed the factors they considered important for the success of those programs. Here are the top five answers:

1. Awareness of federal laws
2. Personal commitment of the chief executive officer
3. Goals and timetables
4. Equal-employment-opportunity policy
5. Analysis of the company's utilization of women[16]

All but one of these answers (number 2) refers to a specific affirmative action policy. Another study showed that federal contractors registered higher gains for minorities and women if they were under review by OFCCP than those contractors that had not been checked.[17] Clearly, pressure from the government does make a difference.

A woman executive summed up her feelings about the need for affirmative action. "Affirmative action is like having a college degree," she said. "It may not help you to do the job, but a woman wouldn't get the job without it."[18]

GOALS—QUOTAS IN DISGUISE?

Companies convicted of civil rights violations are occasionally ordered to meet a quota of minority or female workers as part of the court's judgment. The quota must be met by a certain date or penalties will be given. Goals, on the other hand, are estimates of the numbers a company aspires to achieve in a given time period. All federal contractors must file written reports of goals and timetables under Executive Order 11246. If a goal is not met, the contractor must report the company's good-faith efforts to find or promote members of the targeted groups.

Those are the laws as they appear on the books. But is that the way they are in real life? Is a "goal" any different from a "quota"? Is 25 percent actually something to aim for rather than an amount to be achieved or else? Critics would answer no to these questions, but supporters firmly give the opposite reply. To supporters of affirmative action, goals are not only distinct from quotas but also an excellent means of achieving equality. According to supporters, goals are much more flexible than quotas. They cite one study that showed that while most affirmative action companies increase their representation of minorities and women, only about 10 percent actually achieve the full amount of their stated goals.[19] Supporters also point out that businesses in many surveys have rejected quotas while supporting the idea of goals. This may be because most companies use goals for just about every aspect of business—production for July, sales during the next quarter, etc. As William McEwen of Monsanto Company said, "We're accustomed to setting goals. Business has always set objectives."[20] Added economist Barbara Bergman from the University of Maryland, "The only way management can understand whether a program is effective or not is through statistics."[21] Goals help companies "set sights on a target and develop strategies to achieve it," explained one executive from Coors Brewing Company.[22]

DOES AFFIRMATIVE ACTION HARM
THOSE IT IS SUPPOSED TO HELP?

In the summer of 1987, the New York Yankees hired Chris Chambliss, a former player, as a coach. This was shortly after Al Campanis made his remarks about blacks in baseball and the major leagues began an affirmative action program. The news media questioned Chambliss, a black man, closely. Did he get his job because of race? Chambliss's answer was firm: He got the job, he said, because he knows baseball.

A reaction similar to that of the media seems to follow almost everyone who is among the first of a particular race or sex in each career or school. Critics see this as one of the drawbacks of affirmative action, but supporters say that it is not really a problem. According to supporters of affirmative action, after someone shows that he or she can do the job, negative comments from colleagues die down, and respect replaces resentment.

With those who are not colleagues of affirmative-action employees or students, it may be a different story. Many Americans seem to have a general feeling that "those people" have gotten the upper hand. As one student said, "It's much easier for a woman or a black to get into medical school these days than it is for a white man."[23] Affirmative action supporters point out, however, that statistics do not back up this attitude. White men still earn more than minorities and women and still occupy proportionally more places in professional schools (for medicine, law, business, etc.) than any other group. Furthermore, supporters feel that many affirmative action programs have actually benefitted whites. Brian Weber, for example, was disappointed when he was not accepted for Kaiser's training program. However, before affirmative action became a serious consideration, there was no training program in his company at all, even though the union had long requested one. The whites who did join the program reaped rewards from a program that black pressure had brought about. The way to combat negative attitudes, supporters say, is to insist on the truth, not to drop affirmative action programs because of a false assumption.

There is also little evidence that affirmative action hurts the self-image of blacks, other minorities, or women. In a 1978 Harvard study, fewer than 5 percent of the black students enrolled there said that they had moderate to severe doubts about their own academic ability. Over 75 percent had no doubts at all. Sixty percent of the white Harvard students questioned said they had "no doubts" about their black classmates' ability.[24] Supporters add that to be deprived of jobs or education would be far more harmful to one's self-image than any affirmative action program.

Martin Luther King, Jr., once commented that the civil rights movement had helped blacks claim the right to sit together with whites at a lunch counter. However, King added, if blacks had no money to buy food, that right was meaningless. Affirmative action supporters feel that these programs are an attempt to make the ideal of equality into a concrete reality. With better education and jobs, minorities and women will be able to buy lunch—not with handouts but with their own money.

6

THE CASE
AGAINST
AFFIRMATIVE
ACTION

The speaker, a district attorney in a major American city, proudly explained her accomplishments to a high school audience. "Since I took office," she said, "there are more female assistant D.A.s than ever before. I have appointed three women as division heads." Later she added, "I hope to see a woman president in my lifetime."

Almost immediately hands were raised. "Shouldn't you hope for a qualified person to be elected—regardless of gender?" challenged one student.

"Did you hire those assistant district attorneys just because they were female?" inquired another.

"Would you hire a woman instead of a man with more experience?" added a third questioner.

"Those are very complicated questions," answered the speaker.[1] Before she could go on, she was cut off by the roar of the crowd. Aha, they seemed to say, we caught you.

The idea underlying these students' reaction is that merit should be the only consideration in the hiring process. Look for the best man for the job, they believe, and if that "man" turns out to be a woman, fine. If a black is the most qualified, the black should be employed. If not, the black must look elsewhere.

These students' beliefs are part of a long American tradition. When the early colonists emigrated from Europe, they left behind a society in which birth into a particular social class largely determined an individual's success in life. There was little hope for the children of a peasant or a shopkeeper to be anything more than their parents had been. But America was different. Here everyone could start off on more or less equal footing and rise as high as individual desire and ability allowed. As the nineteenth-century American philosopher Ralph Waldo Emerson wrote, America issues "an invitation to every nation, to every race and skin . . . equal laws to all. Let them compete, and success to the strongest, the wisest, and the best."[2]

At least that was the ideal. In practice, there were always exceptions. The most notable, of course, are blacks, who were brought to America in slavery. Among other groups, immigrants who had wealth and status in the "old country" started out here with an advantage. So did any American who had friends or relatives in the power structure.

There have been many attempts to level these advantages and promote the idea of merit. In the early nineteenth century, the civil service system was established for federal jobs. Later, similar systems were created in many states and counties for local jobs. In the civil service system job applicants take tests, and only those who pass are considered for employment. Hiring is done according to scores, with those whose marks are the best receiving the first offers. There are some exceptions to this; veterans, for example, receive extra points as a reward for service to the nation. The tests are supposed to ensure that only the most qualified people are hired.

In the 1960s, the civil rights movement also used the idea

of merit as one of its arguments. Speakers continually referred to "equal opportunity"—the opportunity for minority groups to compete freely with whites and to be judged, as Martin Luther King, Jr., said, "not by the color of their skin but by the content of their character."

Critics charge that these civil rights ideals shifted when affirmative action programs were instituted. Instead of equality of opportunity, they say, affirmative action promotes equality of result. At times, civil service scores are not strictly followed, and job applicants with more experience or skills are passed over in order to achieve racial or gender balance. Proportional numbers become the goal, not fairness, and the American ideal of merit gets lost in the shuffle.

LOWERED QUALITY?

After a court order requiring increased hiring and promotion of minority candidates, a white firefighter in Cleveland, Ohio, complained, "Who is going to be leading me into a fire: a highly-qualified person or someone who got there by the color of his skin?"[3] The firefighter voiced the fears of many people—fears that affirmative action will lower the quality of American products or services. After all, opponents ask, if the highest-scoring civil service applicants are not hired or if students with lower-than-usual grades are accepted into top universities, how can standards be maintained?

There are some troubling statistics behind these charges. On the average, minority students do score lower than whites on standardized written tests such as the SAT, the Graduate Record Examination, and many civil service tests.[4] There are many theories about the reasons for this: differences in life experience, lower-quality schools, cultural bias in the tests themselves, and so forth. Critics of affirmative action believe that these are the problems that must be addressed first, before employment or college entrance is considered. Promoting or accepting people who are not qualified is not the answer, they maintain, and doing so may be harmful to society.

Opponents also say that some jobs are simply not suitable for women and never will be. The body of the average woman is smaller than that of the average man. On some physical tests, such as those for firefighters, applicants must carry body-sized loads at a rapid pace to simulate a rescue. Far fewer women than men pass this type of test. To change the test so that more women qualify, opponents claim, is to lower standards and to put society in danger.

Recently, a federal appeals court agreed. In New York City the test for firefighters had been changed because almost no women were able to pass the original version and supporters of affirmative action claimed that the test did not really measure firefighting skills. The revised test was challenged, and the court ruled that "the Fire Department is entitled to select those who are endowed with the physical abilities to act effectively in the first moments at a fire scene, where immediate speed and strength literally concern matters of life and death."[5] Opponents of affirmative action believe that the court decision states an obvious truth: Natural differences cannot be ignored or legislated away without a sacrifice in quality.

Furthermore, some personnel or admissions officers feel pressure to produce an increase in minority and female candidates, whether or not there are enough fully qualified applicants. Several faculty members of Cornell University wrote to the *New York Times* in 1972 that their university president interpreted affirmative action to mean "the hiring of additional minority persons and females" even if they were "unqualified or marginally qualified."[6] A 1973 survey of 162 chairmen of university sociology departments found that 44 felt obliged to hire a woman or minority "regardless of whether or not he or she was the best candidate for the job."[7] In 1988, Duke University's Faculty Advisory Council voted to require each department to hire one additional black teacher by 1993. Critics, who pointed out that in 1987 only 6 blacks received Ph.D.'s in math, feared that less-qualified teachers might be hired just to fulfill the requirements of the Faculty Advisory Council.[8]

STATISTICS AND DISCRIMINATION

Anyone watching a professional basketball game will notice that a great many players are members of minority groups—far more than the proportion of those groups in American society. Similarly, 94 percent of all nurses are female. Does this mean that white basketball players have been discriminated against or that males have been kept out of nursing? Of course not, exclaim opponents of affirmative action. In their view, tradition, individual preference, and job qualifications have determined the racial and gender proportions of many jobs, not discrimination. There is no guarantee, they explain, that the career interests of Americans will be distributed in the same proportions as the U.S. population. As Supreme Court Justice Antonin Scalia commented in the Johnson case (in which a woman was promoted to dispatcher), the lack of women in road construction work was probably not due to prejudice but rather resulted from "long-standing social attitudes . . . [in which construction] . . . has not been regarded by women themselves as desirable work."[9]

Furthermore, opponents feel that requiring this type of representation is unrealistic. One critic pointed out that there are simply not enough black Ph.D.s to give every university a proper proportion of black professors. A building inspector in Milwaukee, charged with changing the racial and gender makeup of his work force, complained, "There isn't one female plumber that we know of."[10]

Artificial goals for the number of women and minorities in a particular job do not promote civil rights, opponents charge. Rather, they are an attempt at social engineering. Another Supreme Court justice, the late William O. Douglas, summed up this point of view. He stated that the Constitution "commands the elimination of racial barriers, not their creation in order to satisfy our theory as to how society ought to be organized."[11]

SELF-IMAGE AND REPUTATION

A few years ago former Secretary of the Interior James Watt described a coal-leasing board he had appointed as having "a black, a woman, two Jews, and a cripple."[12] Watt was widely criticized and eventually lost his job because of these and other remarks. However, some people believe that Watt's comment illustrates one of the dangers of affirmative action programs. By allowing race, religion, sex, or ethnic group to be a factor in education or employment, affirmative action may present the image that it is the only factor in an individual's success. This may lead to resentment on the part of other workers and may actually increase racial or sexual prejudice. Clarence Pendleton, head of the U.S. Commission on Civil Rights under President Reagan, stated, "Affirmative action takes away from legitimate minority success. People look at the black banker downtown who has made it on his own and say, 'He got his job because of affirmative action.' "[13] A 1988 Gallup poll asked people to respond to this statement: "While some blacks benefit in work or school from preference over equally qualified whites, some people may feel the achievements of these blacks are not fully earned." Thirty-eight percent of blacks polled felt that this was a "very serious" problem; an additional 35 percent of blacks and 53 percent of whites felt it was a "somewhat serious" problem.[14]

Others charge that affirmative action encouraged a negative self-image in the very groups it is designed to help. They believe that such programs are based on the assumption that women and minorities cannot achieve on their own. In the words of Linda Chavez, former director of the U.S. Commission on Civil Rights, affirmative action implies that "women are the weaker sex and need special protections in order to be able to compete."[15]

DOES IT WORK?

Does affirmative action do what it is supposed to? Does it actually help disadvantaged workers get a better share of the American dream? Some people think that the answer to this question is a resounding no. True, statistics do show that minorities and women have entered fields previously closed to them and have increased their salaries in the past twenty years. But, critics say, these gains are not necessarily attributable to affirmative action programs. Thomas Sowell, a black scholar and staunch opponent of these plans, argues that blacks were making remarkable progress even before the institution of affirmative action programs. In the hundred years following the end of slavery, he says, blacks rose from conditions found only in the poorest of Third World countries to relative comfort. Today's black secretary or mechanic, Sowell says, represents a great deal of progress in a historically short span of time. This progress continued after the Civil Rights Act of 1964 and other laws, but, Sowell believes, this is because of black ability and effort rather than legislation.[16] In a 1988 survey 50 percent of blacks and 80 percent of whites said that in spite of past discrimination, blacks should not "receive preference over equally qualified whites in getting into college or getting jobs."[17]

The real beneficiaries of affirmative action, many critics think, are the lawyers and federal employees who design affirmative action programs, sue or defend clients in court, or read the mountains of paperwork every affirmative action study requires. Michael Horowitz, a lawyer for the Office of Management and Budget during the Reagan years, commented that in administering affirmative action, the government "fed big . . . law firms and an enormous bureaucracy but was of little benefit to minorities and women."[18] An essayist also remarked that "a generation of regulation writers has made careers out of defining, structuring, and overseeing numerical racial measures."[19]

Other critics cite the amount of paperwork affirmative action generates. There are a great number of forms and reports that must be made, filled out, and reviewed. A compliance report for a large company may be several inches thick and weigh two or three pounds—and still not be detailed enough. Affirmative action studies are also expensive; a review of a large factory can cost several hundred thousand dollars. The University of Michigan once spent $350,000 compiling statistics.[20] Again, critics feel that too often the purpose of all this paper is to satisfy the government, not to really improve the lives of minorities and women.

WHO BENEFITS?

Do the people who really need help actually receive the benefits of affirmative action? Not necessarily, according to critics. One study showed that 13.5 percent of Italian-

Americans hold professional jobs, as do 14.1 percent of Irish-Americans and 14.8 percent of German-Americans. These groups are not covered by affirmative action. On the other hand, 15.2 percent of blacks from the West Indies were professionals even before affirmative action began— and West Indians are eligible for the programs.[21] Other opponents point out that all members of certain groups are qualified to join affirmative action plans regardless of their economic background or life experience. Like President Reagan, these people believe that only actual victims of discrimination deserve help.

Others object to the method of racial classification. Currently, people simply identify their own race or ethnic group. However, some critics foresee great competition for membership in affirmative action as the programs promise even more benefits and better jobs. This may make an official system of racial classification necessary—a step that seems old-fashioned and racist. Most people applauded in 1985 when the state of Louisiana repealed an old law defining "colored" as someone who is $1/32$ Negro.[22] Yet critics charge that this law may have to be reinstated as more people compete for multimillion-dollar set-asides or top professional jobs.

Outright fraud is another problem that has already arisen. In fact, Hollywood has even made a movie about it! In *Soul Man,* a young student who cannot afford to attend Harvard darkens his face in order to qualify for a minority scholarship. In real life, a few companies that were actually owned and operated by white males listed women or minorities as the "official" owners. The companies were then eligible for set-asides or other benefits. A Pennsylvania company, RJD, was prosecuted in 1985 for charges that the owner, a black man, fronted for several white corporations and obtained $8 million worth of government contracts. In Missouri, a minority company was accused of falsely obtaining over $3 million in contracts under affirmative action regulations. Opponents feel that this type of fraud will increase as the number of affirmative action benefits grow.[23]

WHO PAYS THE PRICE?

Fraud may cost the American taxpayers money, but there is another cost to affirmative action, according to some observers. Whenever one person receives a job, another does not. Each promotion is accompanied by someone else's failure to get a better job. With affirmative action, critics say, that cost is borne by white males—even those who may be personally innocent of racism or sexism in their own lives.

Opponents feel that this is not only unfair but also unconstitutional. They point to Article III of the U.S. Constitution, which specifically forbids "corruption of blood." Corruption of blood is the punishment of descendants for the wrongdoings of their ancestors. According to this view, reverse discrimination against a particular white male today is actually punishment for discrimination committed by someone else. The guilty parties may not even be related. A Brooklyn College professor reported this exchange about affirmative action in his classroom: A black student charged, "My great-grandfather was a slave! You owe me!" A Jewish student replied, "My great-grandfather was in a Polish ghetto when yours was a slave! I don't owe you anything!"[24] Orrin Hatch, a conservative Republican senator from Utah, expressed the same idea after the Supreme Court's Weber decision. (Weber had been passed over for a training program in favor of a black with less seniority.) "It's pretty tough to convince Mr. Weber that that's fair because maybe 100 years ago one of his ancestors or somebody's ancestors discriminated against blacks," Hatch stated.[25] Antonin Scalia noted that reverse discrimination often affects those near the bottom of the economic scale, those he calls "unknown, unaffluent [not rich], unorganized."[26]

USING ALCOHOL
TO TREAT ALCOHOLISM

A witty magazine columnist once said that affirmative action is when the court orders you to stop discriminating and start reverse discriminating. Linking these two ideas illustrates perhaps the most important objection to affirmative action. To some people, these programs appear just as racist and sexist as the injustices they are designed to remedy. They view discrimination for a "good" reason as just as terrible as discrimination for a "bad" reason.

Other opponents label affirmative action as "the new racism." According to this theory, affirmative action denies women and minorities the right to compete as equals; indeed, it actually assumes that they cannot compete. It treats these groups as commodities instead of people; every office must have its supply of pencils, typewriters, minorities, and women. When supporters of affirmative action programs claim that this discrimination is necessary to make up for past injustices, critics answer with the proverb "Two wrongs don't make a right." Or, as an attorney in the Justice Department during the Reagan administration commented, "You can't use alcohol to treat alcoholism."[27]

Eleven high school students may have summed up this position the best of all. The students were all semifinalists in the Westinghouse Science Talent Search—a prestigious contest—and they were all Asian-Americans. After reading several articles praising their scientific success and examin-

ing its relation to their ethnic background, the students protested. "All of us are proud of our ethnicity," they wrote in
a letter to the *New York Times,* "but we are concerned that
whenever a group of people is given wide attention . . . there
is a danger of losing the individuality of each person in that
group. Such labeling leads to . . . prejudice . . . a disease that
can never be cured by science."[28]

7

THE FUTURE
OF AFFIRMATIVE
ACTION

On October 19, 1987, panic swept through Wall Street. The floor of the New York Stock Exchange, normally hectic, began to resemble a mad tea party. Shares in many of the nation's businesses were being traded at a furious pace, and prices were falling with record-breaking speed. Investors, it seemed, had lost confidence in the economy. By the day's end the Dow-Jones average, an indication of stock prices, was 508 points lower than it had been on the previous day. Some observers took to calling October 19 Black Monday, a reference to the Black Tuesday of 1929 that ushered in the Great Depression.

In the weeks that followed Black Monday, the market took a mini-roller coaster ride as stock prices nervously climbed and fell. Unemployment was low, and many economic signs were positive, but pessimists pointed out that this was also the case after the 1929 stock crash. Economic experts worked overtime trying to understand the meaning of these events. To this date, no one is completely sure what the long-range effect of October 19 will be. Many analysts foresee a long period of recession (a slowing of the econ-

The New York Stock Exchange on October 19, 1987,
a day that became known as Black Monday for
the record-breaking speed with which stock prices
fell. Although that hectic day is over, its effects
are still being felt in the economy.

omy), and a few even envision a depression in the early 1990s. If either of these predictions comes true, the affirmative action debate is likely to become even more heated. When times are hard and unemployment rises, competition for jobs is fierce. White male workers may resent programs that give members of other groups an extra edge. At the same time, minorities and women, who are usually the most recent entrants to the work force, may suffer from "last hired, first fired" layoffs.

If there are cutbacks in funds for public works because of a slow economy, there may be other pressures on affirmative action as more firms compete for contracts. Women and minorities may even be pitted against each other as both groups share affirmative action set-asides. In fact, there have already been a few disputes of this kind. In 1987, women were included for the first time in the 10 percent set-asides for federally financed highway projects. In Chicago, firms headed by women have won nearly three times as much of the contract money for the repair of an expressway as black-owned businesses. Many blacks are bitter about this. Ralph C. Thomas III, executive director of the National Association of Minority Contractors, commented, "It's ridiculous to consider women as minorities."[1] But Kim Gundy of the National Association of Women said, "Women have been a disadvantaged group when it comes to construction business."[2]

Politics will also be a factor in the future of affirmative action. Ronald Reagan's opposition to the programs shaped the policy of the Justice Department during his presidency; many observers believe that enforcement of existing affirmative action laws slackened in the 1980s. George Bush and Michael Dukakis in the 1988 race had to answer questions about their views on affirmative action because it is an important issue to many voters. Also, the new president will have the power to write or retract executive orders. Executive Order 11246 and the other orders that form the legal basis for much of affirmative action will be subject to change if the new president desires it.

In any case, many executives believe that affirmative action will be a part of business life in America for some time to come. In a survey taken in the mid-1980s, 122 major companies said that they would "use numerical objectives [goals] to track the progress of women and minorities . . . regardless of the government regulations." Only 6 said that they would drop their affirmative action programs if those programs were not required.[3] As one insurance executive put it, "It's become the way we do business."[4] Many observers also believe that affirmative action is an established custom in education; admissions officers will probably continue to consider race or sex as one factor in the decision to accept or reject a candidate.

All affirmative action plans will still be subject to legal guidelines determined by the Supreme Court. The court ruled on one affirmative action case during the 1987–88 term. *Watson* v. *Fort Worth Bank and Trust* was an appeal by a former bank teller. The teller, a black woman, claimed that the bank promoted white workers to supervisory positions, while black tellers with more seniority were passed over. The teller used statistics showing the number of blacks and whites in each type of job and the employees' years of experience to prove discrimination.

The Justice Department argued on behalf of the bank, stating that statistics alone are not sufficient proof of discrimination. The department's position is that employees who believe they have been discriminated against must prove that their employer intended to discriminate. The opposition argued that this standard will make it much harder for women and minorities to establish proof of discrimination and the need for affirmative action programs.[5] In June 1988, the court voted 8-0 in favor of the bank teller. Justice Kennedy, who was not a member of the court when the case was argued, did not vote.

During the 1988-89 term, the court will judge the case of the *City of Richmond* v. *J. A. Croson Company.* This case concerns set-asides. Richmond, Virginia, like thirty-two states and many local governments, reserves some of its public works contracts for minority firms. The city council began this program in 1983 to counteract what it considered a long history of discrimination against minorities in city construction projects. Under one of the terms of the plan, white-owned firms that receive business from the city must subcontract at least 30 percent of the value of the contract to minority businesses. A white-owned firm sued the city, claiming that no discrimination was ever proved against the city and that the affirmative action program was therefore not justified. The lower court ruled against the city, but Richmond appealed to the Supreme Court for reinstatement of its set-aside program.[6]

The court will also hear the case of *Martin* v. *Wilks, Personnel Board of Jefferson County.* White firefighters and other city employees have challenged a court order that provides promotions for blacks. According to the white plaintiffs, the court order allows the promotion of less-qualified blacks.[7] The arguments over affirmative action will continue. Even the most fervent supporters of the programs acknowledge that they are really temporary measures— Band-Aids applied to the wounds of racism and sexism that must be removed when healing is complete. When will that be? No one knows, but the day when a color-blind society is achieved and affirmative action programs are abolished will probably be the only possible end to the debate.

NOTES

Chapter One

1. Evan Thomas, "Assault on Affirmative Action," *Time,* February 25, 1985, p. 19.
2. Richard F. America, "Rethinking Affirmative Action in Banks," *The Bankers Magazine,* January/February 1984, p. 83.
3. James J. Kilpatrick, "Still More Equal Than Others," *Nation's Business,* April 1984, p. 4.
4. "Negative Action," *Nation,* June 30, 1984, p. 788.
5. Charles Murray, "Affirmative Racism," *New Republic,* December 31, 1984, p. 18.
6. Robert Drinan, "Another Look at Affirmative Action," *America,* February 9, 1985, p. 105.
7. Harvey C. Mansfield, "The Underhandedness of Affirmative Action," *National Review,* May 4, 1984, p. 26.
8. Thomas Nagel, "Caste Struggle," *New Republic,* January 23, 1984, p. 14.
9. Lori B. Miller, "Medical Schools Adding to Efforts on Minorities," *New York Times,* August 3, 1987, p. II-3.
10. Drinan, p. 106.
11. Author interview.
12. "Class Trains Minority Group Members as Arbitrators," *New York Times,* June 28, 1987, p. 42.
13. "Class Trains . . . Arbitrators," p. 42.
14. "Class Trains . . . Arbitrators," p. 42.

15. Bernie Lee, "Mothers, Let Your Children Grow Up to Be Correction Officers," *Chinese for Affirmative Action Newsletter,* Spring/Summer 1987, p. 5.
16. Letter from Miro Todorovich to Howard Glickstein, quoted in *Reverse Discrimination,* edited by Barry R. Gross (Buffalo, N.Y.: Prometheus, 1977), p. 21.
17. Douglas B. Huron, "Affirmative Action: It's Useful," *Current,* February 1985, p. 28.
18. Huron, p. 28.
19. M. K. Guzda, "Surpassing Its Goals," *Editor and Publisher,* July 28, 1984, p. 9.
20. Frank Litsky, "Affirmative Action Plan Is Started in Baseball," *New York Times,* July 5, 1987, p. S3.
21. Esther Iverem, "Blacks Settle Bias Suit Filed Against LIRR and 14 Unions," *New York Times,* July 6, 1987, p. 33.
22. Michael Quint, "A Black Firm's Wall St. Rise," *New York Times,* August 29, 1987, p. D1.
23. James Farmer, "Where Does the Civil Rights Movement Stand Today?" *The Humanist,* November/December 1985, p. 6.

Chapter Two

1. Bradwell v. Illinois 16–130 (1873).
2. Sharon Whitney, *The Equal Rights Amendment* (New York: Franklin Watts, 1984), p. 18.
3. Whitney, p. 15.
4. Lois W. Banner, *Women in Modern America: A Brief History,* 2nd ed. (New York: Harcourt Brace Jovanovich, 1984), p. 202.
5. Whitney, p. 36.
6. Whitney, p. 36.
7. Banner, p. 219.
8. Banner, p. 223.
9. Banner, p. 36.
10. Banner, p. 163.
11. Tom Goldstein, "Women in the Law Aren't Equal Yet," *New York Times,* February 12, 1988, p. B7.
12. Ann Morrison, Randall P. White, Ellen Van Velsor, *Breaking the Glass Ceiling* (Reading, Mass.: Addison-Wesley, 1987), p. 20.
13. Andrea Adelson, "Women Still Finding Bias in Engineering," *New York Times,* March 9, 1988, p. D6.
14. Gilda Berger, *Women, Work, and Wages,* (New York: Franklin Watts, 1986), p. 68.
15. Berger, p. 69.
16. Berger, p. 66.

17. Berger, p. 5.
18. "Balancing Act," *Time,* April 6, 1987, p. 20.
19. Berger, p. 24.
20. Berger, p. 29.
21. "Status of Women Rises but Pay Lags, Study Finds," *New York Times,* July 22, 1987, p. A23.
22. Berger, p. 32.
23. "Status of Women," p. A23.
24. "Status of Women," p. A23.
25. Whitney, p. 4.
26. Richard F. America, "Rethinking Affirmative Action in Banks," *Bankers Magazine,* January/February 1984, p. 81.
27. Alphonso Pinkney, *Black Americans* (Englewood Cliffs, N.J.: Prentice-Hall, 1969), pp. 3–5.
28. Leslie Dunbar, *Minority Report* (New York: Pantheon, 1984), p. 121.
29. "Negro in America," *Encyclopedia Americana,* p. 68.
30. Harry Ashmore, *Hearts and Minds* (New York: McGraw-Hill, 1982), p. 13.
31. William Harris, *The Harder We Run* (London: Oxford University Press, 1982), p. 7.
32. Pinkney, p. 23.
33. Harris, p. 9.
34. Elaine Pascoe, *Racial Prejudice* (New York: Franklin Watts, 1985), p. 28.
35. Ashmore, p. 168.
36. Ashmore, p. 168.
37. Harris, p. 39.
38. Harris, p. 40.
39. Harris, p. 101.
40. Harris, p. 105.
41. Dunbar, p. 157.
42. Dunbar, p. 179.
43. Joel Dreyfuss and Charles Lawrence III, *The Bakke Case* (New York: Harcourt Brace Jovanovich, 1979), pp. 142–43.
44. Edward Fiske, "Integration Lags at Public Schools," *New York Times,* July 26, 1987, p. 1.
45. Edward Fiske, "Colleges Open New Minority Drives," *New York Times,* November 18, 1987, p. II-6.
46. Julie Johnson, "Further Decline in Minority Enrollment Is Feared," *New York Times,* January 20, 1988, p. B8.
47. Ted Gest, "Why the Drive on Job Bias Is Still Going Strong," *U.S. News and World Report,* June 17, 1985, p. 67.
48. Dunbar, p. 61.

49. Dunbar, p. 61.
50. Tom Wicker, "Always With Us," *New York Times,* November 19, 1987, p. A31.
51. "Face Up to Race," *New York Times,* September 30, 1987, p. A30.
52. Herbert L. Marx, Jr., *The American Indian* (New York: Wilson, 1973), p. 24.
53. Alvin M. Josephy, Jr., *Now That the Buffalo's Gone* (New York: Knopf, 1982), pp. 142–50.
54. Josephy, p. 129.
55. Josephy, pp. 131–32.
56. Pascoe, p. 64.
57. Kathleen Teltich, "Philanthropy Gives Hope to Oglala," *New York Times,* November 9, 1987, p. 18.
58. Pascoe, p. 83.
59. Jane Claypool, *The Worker in America* (New York: Franklin Watts, 1985), p. 67.
60. Pascoe, p. 74.
61. Claypool, p. 67.
62. Dreyfuss and Lawrence, pp. 106–107.
63. Wicker, p. A31.
64. Author from phone conversation with the Bureau of Labor Statistics.
65. Fiske, "Integration Lags," p. 1.
66. Wayne Moquin and Charles Van Doren, *A Documentary History of the Mexican-American* (New York: Praeger, 1971), p. 200.
67. Moquin and Van Doren, pp. 295–96.
68. Nathan Glazer and Daniel P. Moynihan, *Beyond the Melting Pot* 2nd ed. (Cambridge, Mass.: MIT Press, 1970), p. 115.
69. Glazer and Moynihan, p. 115.
70. Herbert Hammerman, *A Decade of New Opportunity* (Washington, D.C.: Potomac Institute, 1984), p. 40.

Chapter Three

1. Herbert Hammerman, *A Decade of New Opportunity* (Washington, D.C.: Potomac Institute, 1984), p. 11.
2. Hammerman, p. 11.
3. "Affirmative Facts," *Commonweal,* June 21, 1985, p. 357.
4. Joel Dreyfuss and Charles Lawrence III, *The Bakke Case* (New York: Harcourt Brace Jovanovich, 1979), p. 237.
5. Paul Seabury, "HEW and the Universities," *Reverse Discrimination,* edited by Barry R. Gross (Buffalo, N.Y.: Prometheus, 1977), p. 111.
6. Thomas Sowell, "Affirmative Action Reconsidered," *Reverse Discrimination,* edited by Barry R. Gross (Buffalo, N.Y.: Prometheus, 1977), p. 115.

7. Lloyd G. Reynolds, Stanley H. Masters, Colletta H. Moser, *Readings in Labor, Economics, and Labor Relations,* 4th ed. (Englewood Cliffs, N.J.: Prentice-Hall, 1986), p. 207.
8. Seabury, p. 99.
9. Hammerman, p. 13.
10. Hammerman, p. 13.
11. Hammerman, p. 51.
12. Hammerman, p. 7.
13. Hammerman, p. 16.
14. William Harris, *The Harder We Run* (London: Oxford University Press, 1982), pp. 156–57.
15. Bernard E. Anderson, "Affirmative Action Is Economically Necessary," *Social Justice* edited by Bonnie Szumski (St. Paul, Minn.: Greenhaven Press, 1984), p. 46.
16. Shirley S. Fader, "What Are Your Chances of Being Promoted?" *Working Woman,* July 1985, p. 36.
17. Reynolds, Masters, and Moser, p. 213.
18. Hammerman, p. 5.
19. Dreyfuss and Lawrence, pp. 242–48.
20. Dreyfuss and Lawrence, pp. 242–48.
21. Dreyfuss and Lawrence, p. 249.
22. Evan Thomas, "Assault on Affirmative Action," *Time,* February 25, 1985, p. 19.
23. Anne B. Fisher, "Businesses Like to Hire by the Numbers," *Fortune,* September 16, 1985, p. 27.
24. David C. Ruffin, "Erasing Civil Rights: the Onslaught Continues," *Black Enterprise,* November 1985, p. 29.
25. Ruffin, p. 29.
26. Ruffin, p. 29.
27. Daniel B. Moskowitz, "A New Drive to Reorganize Equal Opportunity," *Business Week,* March 11, 1985, p. 42.
28. Ted Gest, "Why the Drive on Job Bias is Still Going Strong," *US News and World Report,* June 17, 1985, p. 67.
29. Aric Press, "The New Rights War," *Newsweek,* December 30, 1985, p. 67.
30. "From Action to Outreach," *The Economist,* January 5, 1985, p. 17.

Chapter Four

Note: All quotes in this chapter, unless otherwise indicated, come from the Supreme Court records of the case. Most large libraries have these records, filed by year. The notes below give the year and number of each case.

1. 401-424 (1971)
2. 438-265 (1978)
3. 443-193 (1979)
4. 448-448 (1980)
5. 467-561 (1984)
6. 106-1842 (1986)
7. 106-3019 (1986)
8. 106-3063 (1986)
9. 106-3331 (1986)
10. 85-1129 (1987)
11. "On Giving Women a Break," *New York Times,* March 27, 1987, p. 30.
12. William Harris, *The Harder We Run* (London: Oxford University Press, 1982), p. 159.
13. Harris, p. 164.
14. Joel Dreyfuss and Charles Lawrence III, *The Bakke Case* (New York: Harcourt Brace Jovanovich, 1979), p. 252.
15. Douglas S. McDowell, *The 1986 Affirmative Action Trilogy* (Washington, D.C.: National Foundation for the Study of Equal Employment Policy, 1986), p. 53.
16. McDowell, p. 53.
17. Samantha Haidt, "Anger and Elation at Ruling on Affirmative Action," *New York Times,* March 29, 1987, p. IV-1.
18. Stuart Taylor, "Ideological Feud Erupts in a Key Appeals Court," *New York Times,* August 15, 1987, p. 7.
19. 86-1415 (1988)
20. "Answers from Judge Kennedy on His Last Day Before Senate Committee," *New York Times,* December 12, 1987, p. B5.

Chapter Five

1. Edmund Newton, "Affirmative Action: Correcting Job Bias," *Black Enterprise,* March 1984, p. 19.
2. Newton, p. 19.
3. Wanda Berry, "Affirmative Action is Just," *Social Justice,* edited by Bonnie Szumski (St. Paul, Minn.: Greenhaven Press, 1984), p. 20.
4. R. M. O'Neill, "The Case for Preferential Admissions," *Reverse Discrimination,* edited by Barry R. Gross (Buffalo, N.Y.: Prometheus, 1977), p. 81.
5. Anne B. Fisher, "Businesses Like to Hire by the Numbers," *Fortune,* September 16, 1985, p. 27.
6. Claire Safran, "Corporate Women: Just How Far Have We Come?" *Working Women,* March 1984, p. 99.

7. Mark Starr, "Attacking Affirmative Action," *Newsweek,* May 13, 1985, p. 39.
8. Safran, p. 99.
9. Safran, p. 99.
10. Edward J. Erler, "Brown v. Board of Education at 30," *National Review,* September 7, 1984, p. 30.
11. M. K. Guzda, "Making Affirmative Action Work," *Editor and Publisher,* June 8, 1985, p. 17.
12. "Whites Found Least Likely to Hire Minorities," *New York Times,* September 20, 1987, p. 28.
13. Berry, p. 20.
14. Peggy Simpson, "Affirmative Action in Action," *Working Women,* March 1984, p. 105.
15. Bernard Anderson, "Affirmative Action Is Economically Necessary," *Social Justice,* edited by Bonnie Szumski (St. Paul, Minn.: Greenhaven Press, 1984), p. 46.
16. Lloyd G. Reynolds, Stanley H. Masters, Colletta H. Moser, *Readings in Labor, Economics, and Labor Relations* (Englewood Cliffs, N.J.: Prentice-Hall, 1986), p. 212.
17. Herbert Hammerman, *A Decade of New Opportunity* (Washington, D.C.: Potomac Institute, 1984), p. 43.
18. Safran, p. 99.
19. Aric Press, "The New Rights War," *Newsweek,* December 30, 1985, p. 67.
20. Daniel B. Moskowitz, "A New Drive to Reorganize Equal Opportunity," *Business Week,* March 11, 1985, p. 42.
21. Ted Gest, "Why the Drive on Job Bias Is Still Going Strong," *U.S. News and World Report,* June 17, 1985, p. 67.
22. Gest, p. 67.
23. Author interview.
24. Derek Bok, "Admitting Success," *New Republic,* February 4, 1985, p. 15.

Chapter Six

1. Author interview.
2. Nathan Glazer, "The Emergence of an American Ethnic Pattern," *Reverse Discrimination,* edited by Barry R. Gross (Buffalo, N.Y.: Prometheus, 1977), p. 143.
3. Ted Gest, "Affirmative Verdict on Racial Hiring," *US News and World Report,* July 14, 1986, p. 17.
4. Edward Fiske, "Steady Gains Achieved by Blacks on College Admissions Test Scores," *New York Times,* September 23, 1987, p. 1.

5. E. R. Shipp, "Ruling Could Curtail Hiring New Women in the Fire Department," *New York Times,* April 14, 1987, p. 1.
6. Nathan Glazer, *Affirmative Discrimination* (New York: Basic Books, 1975), p. 60.
7. Glazer, *Affirmative Discrimination,* p. 62.
8. "Duke Requires All Departments to Hire Blacks," *New York Times,* April 21, 1988, p. A10.
9. 85-1129 (1987)
10. Ted Gest, "Why the Drive on Job Bias Is Still Going Strong," *U.S. News and World Report,* June 17, 1985, p. 67.
11. 416-312 (1974)
12. Harvey C. Mansfield, Jr. "The Underhandedness of Affirmative Action," *National Review,* May 4, 1984, p. 26.
13. Clarence M. Pendleton, Jr., "Minority Success and Affirmative Action," *Social Justice,* edited by Bonnie Szumski (St. Paul, Minn.: Greenhaven Press, 1984), p. 26.
14. "Black and White: a Newsweek Poll," *Newsweek,* March 7, 1988, p. 23.
15. "Anger and Elation at Ruling on Affirmative Action," *New York Times,* March 29, 1987, p. IV-1.
16. Thomas Sowell, "Affirmative Action: It's Not Progress," *Current,* February 1985, p. 24.
17. "Black and White: a Newsweek Poll," p. 23.
18. David C. Ruffin, "Erasing Civil Rights," *Black Enterprise,* November 1985, p. 29.
19. "AKA Quotas, Continued," *National Review,* December 13, 1985, p. 14.
20. Lloyd G. Reynolds, Stanley H. Masters, Colletta H. Moser, *Readings in Labor, Economics, and Labor Relations* (Englewood Cliffs, N.J.: Prentice-Hall, 1986), p. 210.
21. William R. Beer, "Affirmative Action in Brooklyn—a View from the Trenches," *New Republic,* November 18, 1985, p. 17.
22. Stephen Markman, "Classifying the Races," *National Review,* April 5, 1985, p. 44.
23. Lynette Hazelton, "Fighting Fraud," *Black Enterprise,* November 1986, p. 22.
24. Beer, p. 17.
25. Richard F. America, "Rethinking Affirmative Action in Banks," *Bankers Magazine,* January/February 1984, p. 80.
26. 85-1129 (1987)
27. W. B. Reynolds, "Affirmative Action is Unjust," *Social Justice,* edited by Bonnie Szumski (St. Paul, Minn.: Greenhaven Press, 1984), p. 27.

28. Letter from Irene Eng, et al., *New York Times,* February 12, 1988, p. A30.

Chapter Seven

1. Dirk Johnson, "Minority Contractors Protest Rule That Gives Women Similar Status," *New York Times,* March 4, 1988, p. 1.
2. Johnson, p. 1.
3. Ted Gest, "Why the Drive on Job Bias Is Still Going Strong," *U.S. News and World Report,* June 17, 1985, p. 67.
4. Claire Safran, "Corporate Women: Just How Far Have We Come?" *Working Women,* March 1984, p. 99.
5. 86-6139 (1988).
6. 87-998 (1988).
7. 87-1614 (1988)

FURTHER
READING

Ashmore, Harry. *Hearts and Minds.* New York: McGraw-Hill, 1982.

Berger, Gilda. *Women, Work, and Wages.* New York: Watts, 1986.

Bok, Derek. "Admitting Success," *New Republic* (Feb. 4, 1985): 15.

Burstein, Paul. *Discrimination, Jobs, and Politics.* Chicago: University of Chicago Press, 1985.

Claypool, Jane. *The Worker in America.* New York: Watts, 1985.

Dreyfuss, Joel, and Charles Lawrence. *The Bakke Case.* New York: Harcourt Brace and Jovanovich, 1979.

Drinan, Robert. "Another Look at Affirmative Action," *America* (Feb. 9, 1985): 105.

Dunbar, Leslie. *Minority Report.* New York: Pantheon, 1984.

Fader, Shirley S. "What Are Your Chances of Being Promoted?" *Working Woman* (July 1985): 36.

Farmer, James. "Where Does the Civil Rights Movement Stand Today?" *The Humanist* (Nov. 12, 1985): 6.

Fisher, Anne B. "Businesses Like to Hire by the Numbers," *Fortune* (Sept. 16, 1985): 27.

Gest, Ted. "Affirmative Verdict on Racial Hiring," *U.S. News and World Report* (July 14, 1986): 17.

———. "Why Drive on Job Bias is Still Going Strong," *U.S. News and World Report* (June 17, 1985): 67.

Glazer, Nathan. *Affirmative Discrimination.* New York: Basic Books, 1975.

Gross, Barry R. *Reverse Discrimination.* Buffalo, NY: Prometheus Books, 1977.

Guzda, M.K. "Surpassing Its Goals," *Editor and Publisher* (July 28, 1984): 9.

Hammerman, Herbert. *A Decade of New Opportunity.* Washington, DC: Potomac Institute, 1984.

Harris, William. *The Harder We Run.* London: Oxford University Press, 1982.

Hazelton, Lynnette. "Fighting Fraud," *Black Enterprise* (Nov. 1986): 22.

Huron, Douglas B. "Affirmative Action: It's Useful," *Current* (Feb. 1985): 28.

Josephy, Alvin, Jr. *Now That the Buffalo's Gone.* New York: Knopf, 1982.

Kilpatrick, James J. "Still More Equal Than Others," *Nation's Business* (Apr. 1984): 4.

Mansfield, Harvey C., Jr. "The Underhandedness of Affirmative Action," *National Review* (May 4, 1984): 26.

Markman, Stephen. "Classifying the Races," *National Review* (Apr. 5, 1985): 44.

Meer, Jeff. "Accentuate the Affirmative," *Psychology Today* (June 1984): 52.

Moquin, Wayne, and Charles VanDoren. *A Documentary History of Mexican-Americans.* New York: Praeger, 1971.

Morrison, Ann, Randall P. White, and Ellen Van Velsor. *Breaking the Glass Ceiling.* Reading, Mass.: Addison-Wesley, 1987.

Moskowitz, Daniel B. "A New Drive to Reorganize Equal Opportunity," *Business Week* (Mar.11, 1985): 42.

Murray, Charles. "Affirmative Racism," *New Republic* (Dec. 31, 1984): 18.

Nagel, Thomas. "Caste Struggle," *New Republic* (Jan. 23, 1984): 14.

Newton, Edmund. "Affirmative Action: Correcting Job Bias," *Black Enterprise* (March 1984): 19.

Pascoe, Elaine. *Racial Rejudice.* New York: Watts, 1985.

Pinkney, Alphonso. *Black Americans.* Englewood Cliffs, NJ: Prentice-Hall, 1969.

Press, Aric. "The New Rights War," *Newsweek* (Dec. 30, 1985): 67.

Ruffin, David C. "Erasing Civil Rights: The Onslaught Continues," *Black Enterprise* (Nov. 1985): 29.

Safran, Claire. "Corporate Women: Just How Far Have We Come," *Working Women* (March 1984): 99.

Simpson, Peggy. "Affirmative Action in Action," *Working Women* (March 1984): 105.

Sowell, Thomas. "Affirmative Action: It's Not Progress," *Current* (Feb. 1985): 24.

Starr, Mark. "Attacking Affirmative Action," *Newsweek* (May 13, 1985): 39.

Szumski, Bonnie. *Social Justice.* St. Paul, Minn: Greenhaven Press, 1984.

Thomas, Evan. "Assault on Affirmative Action," *Time* (Feb. 25, 1985): 19.

INDEX